Future trends in the law as they affect athletics is obviously a subject of the greatest importance, and the author explains what will undoubtedly develop as a result of legal actions which have taken place in the recent past. This will allow the reader to anticipate events that may develop in this area, and as an administrator or one responsible for athletic activities, he can be better prepared to cope with such changes.

The Appendix includes well over 100 legal actions which have involved athletic activities, or activities closely akin to the athletic situation, which might be precedent-setting in nature. Finally, the Bibliography lists a large number of publications which include specific references to particular situations in which the reader may have an interest.

All in all, this book supplies a source of information that has never before been compiled in this manner; it should provide valuable aid for all individuals who have some responsibility for athletic programs. And it should shed much light on a matter of the utmost importance to school athletic programs—a matter which is unfortunately all too often misunderstood or simply overlooked.

THE LEGAL ASPECTS OF ATHLETICS

THE
LEGAL ASPECTS
OF ATHLETICS

by

ANDREW GRIEVE

Assistant Professor of Physical Education

State University College

at Cortland, New York

SOUTH BRUNSWICK AND NEW YORK:
A. S. BARNES AND COMPANY
LONDON: THOMAS YOSE LOFF LTD

© 1969 by A. S. Barnes and Co., Inc.

Library of Congress Catalogue Card Number: 68-27239

A. S. Barnes and Co., Inc.

Cranbury, New Jersey 08512

Thomas Yoseloff Ltd

108 New Bond St.

London W. 1, England

SBN 498-06852-8

Printed in the United States of America

This book is dedicated to my wife Eva, my sons Douglas and Kevin, and to the many fine friends I have on the staff of the Men's Physical Education Department at the State University College at Cortland.

Acknowledgments

I WOULD LIKE TO ACKNOWLEDGE THE FOLLOWING INDIVIDUALS and organizations, without whose cooperation this book would not have been possible:

Dr. John Jehu, Legal Division, New York State Education Department, Albany, N. Y.

Mr. Bruce Meservery, Bureau of Publications, New York State Education Department, Albany, N. Y.

New York State School Boards' Association, Albany, N. Y.

Mr. Larry Grimes, New York State Public High School Athletic Protection Plan, Schenectady, N. Y.

Mr. Clifford Fagan, National Federation of State High School Athletic Associations, Chicago, Illinois.

American Association of Health, Physical Education and Recreation, Washington, D. C.

National Education Association, Washington, D. C.

Foundation Press, Brooklyn, N. Y.

Appleton-Century-Crofts Publishing Company, New York, N. Y.

A. S. Barnes and Co., Inc., Cranbury, N. J.

Physical Education Newsletter, Croft Publications, New London, Connecticut.

Mr. John L. Griffith, Athletic Journal, Evanston, Illinois.

Also the many state public high school athletic associations and legal divisions of the various state education departments who provided numerous answers to my several questionnaires.

And, finally, Dr. Robert Weber, Chairman of the Men's Physical Education Department at State University College at Cortland, who made available to me his extensive files on athletic administration.

ANDREW GRIEVE

Contents

Acknowledgements   7

Introduction   13

1. *Definition of Terms*   21
    Statutes *vs.* Court Judgments   24

2. *Variation in State Statutes*   26
    Statutes of the Fifty States   28

3. *Supervision and Negligence*   39
    Qualifications of a Supervisor   39
    Foresight   42
    Assumption of Risk   45
    Degree of Skill   47
    Training and Conditioning   49
    Number of Participants and Areas   50
    Assigned Duties   53
    Waiver Forms   56
    Opinions of Others   57
    How to Avoid Liability Suits   58

4. *Medical Aspects and Liability*   60
    Physical Examinations   60
    Release from the Doctor   65
    First Aid   65
    Medical Assistance   69
    Illegal Treatment   70
    Doctors' Legal Liability   72
    Financial Responsibility   74

Weight Control   75
The Role of the Athletic Trainer   78

5. *Equipment and Facilities*   80
    Equipment   80
    Purchase of Equipment   82
    Equipment Finance   84
    Facilities   87
    Unattended Facilities   91

6. *Legal Aspects of Spectator Injuries*   92
    Public or Proprietary Functions   95
    Bleachers and Stands   97
    Attendance at Athletic Contests   98

7. *The Legal Aspects of Transportation*   100
    The Use of Public Funds for Athletic
       Transportation   101
    Foresight in Transportation   102
    Court Decisions on Negligence Claims   103
    Privately Owned Vehicles   108

8. *The Legal Aspects of Insurance*   111
    Liability Insurance   111
    Accident Insurance   115

9. *The Legality of Eligibility Standards
Determined by Local School Officials*   117
    The Eligibility of Married Students   121

10. *Equal Competition*   123

11. *Athletic Awards*   128
    Limitations on Awards   129

12. *The Legal Aspects of State Athletic Associations*   132
    Mutual Legal Aid Pact   134
    The Right to Impose Penalties   135
    Legal Actions Involving Athletic Associations   137

13. *Miscellaneous Legal Problems in Athletics*   144
     Broadcasting Athletic Contests   144
     Teacher Supervision and Assignments   146
     Libel and Slander   147
     Injury to a Coach   149
     Hiring Sports Officials   150
     Payment of Officials   151

14. *Future Trends*   155
     Removal of Immunity   155
     Increase in "Save Harmless" Protection   157
     Increase in the Number of Litigations   157
     Larger Financial Settlements   159
     Increase in Slander and Libel Cases   160
     Results of the Trends   161

APPENDIX A. *List of Legal Actions*   163

APPENDIX B. *Bibliography*   171
     Books   171
     Magazine Articles   172
     Pamphlets   174
     Professional Papers   174
     Remarks   174
     Miscellaneous   175

Index   177

Introduction

HIGH SCHOOL ATHLETICS ARE REPLETE WITH SITUATIONS which may, or have already, resulted in legal actions involving coaches, school officers, school districts, or boards of education. There has been a sufficient number of court cases in this area to support such a contention. All too often, however, studies of this nature are limited to a discussion of negligence. Although it is one of the more important phases in this area, negligence is only one of numerous categories which may be the basis for legal action in athletics.

Why is an understanding of the law and athletics so important? It is only realistic for an individual, or group of individuals, responsible for particular activities to be familiar with the legal restrictions and obligations associated with such activities. All professionals should be familiar with the statutes that have an effect upon their daily occupation. It is doubtful if those associated with the coaching and administration of athletics are as well versed in the legal aspects affecting them as are members of other professions.

As employees of a school district, those responsible for all phases of this program should attempt to guarantee that such a district does not become involved in a lawsuit. In many states the school district does not assume the legal burden of protecting the individual from lawsuits and it is only common sense for the individual to protect himself against such unpleasant situations and, at the same time, the possibility of extensive financial loss. Although it is not the purpose of this book, an individual who adheres to practices that will protect both himself and his school district from legal action will at the same time be providing a safe atmosphere for the participants in the athletic program.

Who should be familiar with this area of the law and athletics? All individuals and groups of individuals who have any relationship with the program should be well versed in the manner in which existing statutes will affect them. This would include the boards of education, school administrators, athletic directors, head coaches, assistant coaches, faculty managers of athletics, doctors, school nurses, athletic trainers, purchasing agents, sport officials, school lawyers and transportation directors. All those who have a responsibility to a league or a division of the State Athletic Association, whether they be classified as school personnel or not, must be familiar with the legal aspects which have an effect upon their groups. All too frequently only the areas of negligence and liability are considered, but the legal aspects of the league and the State Athletic Associations in exerting control over athletics must be a vital part of any such study.

In the eyes of the law, previous decisions are referred to quite extensively during any court action. Court records clearly indicate this to be the situation, as frequent references are made to such previous court decisions. Legal precedents carry a great deal of weight as these would seem to indicate that similar circumstances have occurred in the past and that the court had arrived at a particular decision. These decisions could therefore be applicable in parallel actions. For this reason those court actions which are presented in this text can act as a guide to those involved in any phase of athletics as an indication of decisions which have an influence upon incidents in their programs.

In some instances it will be necessary to refer to actions which do not directly involve athletics, but the facts may be so akin to the athletic situation that the results of the decision could be applicable to athletics. Circumstances in a number of areas, such as physical education, pupil transportation, purchase of school equipment, are parallel to those in athletics and it would be possible for the court, or members of the legal profession, to refer to such and still be within proper bounds.

In a number of instances information gathered on litigations involving athletics was presented strictly from the legal viewpoint. In only an extremely small number of sources was information having a major emphasis on the athletic viewpoint offered, a fact which necessarily limited the scope of such information. Legal jargon will usually leave the coach or the director unimpressed, but when presented in terms with which he is readily familiar the impact is usually more effective. One of the main purposes of this text is to present such information in terms which can be clearly understood by all those concerned with athletics.

Although the importance of legal precedence has been emphasized, it is entirely possible that ensuing actions may not adhere to such precedents. This is not meant to indicate the court can choose to ignore them, but numerous factors must be considered. Although two actions may appear to be identical there may nevertheless be slight variations in circumstances which cause the courts to take a completely opposite view. Minute variations could be a solid basis for not adhering to previous decisions.

Court decisions also involve a considerable amount of individual judgment. Simply because one viewpoint was held in the past does not guarantee that those sitting in judgment in another court at another time are going to come up with the same opinions under similar circumstances. Legal precedence, however, does have much to do with final decisions and is rarely ignored either by the counsel for the plaintiff or the defendant. Such past action can do much to sway the opinion of those judging the case, as it will provide them with at least a guideline. Jury cases are even more uncertain, as there are to be several opinions considered rather than just the one; and the more individuals involved in a decision the less certain the outcome.

The results of several of the legal actions which will be presented might no longer be possible in the states in which the original incident occurred, because there have been numerous changes in the statutes of various states over the past several years. Even though this may be the case, such decisions could still be precedent-setting in nature in those states which still retain the statutes under which original incident and decision took place.

During the past several years there has been a definite change in the attitures toward legal liability for supervisors of activities and the school districts. The tendency has been for the courts to expect a greater assumption of responsibility by school personnel. In some instances this has been indicated through court decisions, thereby setting precedents in this area. In others this assumption of increased responsibility has become a matter of law, as state legislatures have passed statutes to guarantee this. The most recent trend has been the removal of the tenet of immunity for school districts. Considerable information will be presented on this change in attitude, but it is mentioned here to indicate why there may be variations in decisions in the same state where the actions appear to be comparable. The removal of such protection through legislation permits the courts to arrive at decisions which might formerly have been impossible.

It is obvious that variations in interpretations and court actions do occur but the previous information should indicate how this would be possible. In a few instances it might even be possible to find variations in the same legal actions. These are normally not discrepancies but rather

the result of appeals to higher courts. Several such instances will be mentioned in the text. Even though the outcomes of some of the cases presented stand on the court
records as such, it is possible that some of those of recent
vintage could still be reversed if they are appealed to some
higher court.

Existing statutes are considerably different from state
to state. It is rare, if not impossible, to find two states whose
laws affecting the various phases of education would be
completely identical. Many run parallel but minor variations do exist in areas which could have an effect upon
athletics. Transportation, finance of equipment, facilities,
etc., would all offer a range of variations. A number of
diversities exist in statutes affecting immunity, legal responsibility, "save harmless" provisions, and the like.

The law is also a constantly fluctuating situation, but
the only reasonable method of approaching such information would be to do so from the viewpoints and statutes as
they exist at the present time. As mentioned previously,
precedents have considerable weight in determining the
outcome of legal actions. These and existing statutes must
be the basis for any presentation in this area of the legal
aspects of athletics. For this reason the emphasis will be
placed on these two areas; although others will enter the
picture, these would seem to be the most important.

THE LEGAL ASPECTS
OF ATHLETICS

1

Definition of Terms

THERE ARE SEVERAL REASONS WHY AN INDIVIDUAL ASSOCIATED with athletics should clearly understand the meaning of legal terms. The terms included will apply most readily to legal actions which may involve athletic activities. Volumes have been written in defining the plethora of legal terms, but since this book is to be directed mainly to lay persons there should be no necessity of attempting to include terms which would not be applicable. Of prime importance is the fact that such information will provide a better understanding of the material to be presented in the text. If an individual associated with athletics becomes involved as a defendant or a witness in a legal action, he will better comprehend the charges either indicated or implied against himself or one of his co-workers.

Act of God: an accident which is inevitable due to forces of nature and a supervisor could not have eliminated the cause in any way.

Assumption of risk: certain dangers are inherent due to the nature of the activity; a supervisor cannot protect an individual from such dangers and therefore cannot be held responsible; the individual assumes a degree of risk will be involved in the activity before he participates.

Attractive nuisance: a dangerous situation which may at-

132074

tract the attention of an individual, particularly children.

Causative factor: an existing situation which is obviously the main cause of an injury.

Civil action: infringing upon the rights of another individual.

Common law: similar to court judgment; not reduced to statutes but arising from customs and created by judges to meet special problems.

Comparative negligence: when both the individual who is responsible for the activity or facility and the injured party have contributed to the negligent act.

Contributory negligence: although direct action did not cause negligence, a certain action of an individual contributed to the negligent act.

Court judgment: an interpretation of the laws or parts of laws which can set a precedent in similar judgments; judges will often interpret through their own opinions due to a lack of legislation or slow legislative action on pressing problems.

Criminal action: an illegal act against the state or society.

Foreseeability: the individual responsible for the negligent act could have foreseen the danger which existed.

Governmental or public function: a school performing a function directly related to educational pursuit.

Immunity: freedom or protection from legal action; in this area as applicable to governmental units and may include school districts.

Injunction: a formal order issued by a court of law ordering a person or group to perform, or refrain from performing, a specific act.

In loco parentis: in the place of the parent.

Liability: being responsible for a negligent action; legal responsibility not fulfilled.

Litigation: the carrying on of a lawsuit.

Malfeasance: an act which is completely illegal and should not be performed under any circumstances.

Mandatory legislation: laws which require adherence.

Misfeasance: an act which may be performed legally but was done so in an improper manner.

Negligence: not exercising the care which a person of ordinary prudence would exercise under similar circumstances; a lack of positive as well as negative action.

Non-feasance: the lack of performing an act which was obviously necessary; failure to perform one's required duty.

Permissive legislation: laws which are passed to allow certain actions by groups involved; such legislation does not mandate such action but allows the action to be taken if so desired.

Precedent: the utilization of a previous court decision in judging a similar court action with comparable circumstances.

Proprietary function: a school performing a function which is not directly related to educational pursuit but more of a profit-making nature.

Respondea superior: the responsibility of an employer for the negligent acts of his employees.

Safe place legislation: laws which require public buildings, including those owned by school districts, to be free from injury-producing conditions.

Save harmless legislation: legislation which requires or permits the Board of Education to protect teachers from large financial losses in cases involving such claims against the teachers.

Scope of work or responsibility: those responsibilities which are assigned to an individual by his superiors.

Statute: a law created through legislation such as a statute passed by a state legislature.

Tort: that phase of the law which deals with personal and property rights; redress for injuries to such which are neither the result of a crime or a contractual failure.

Unavoidable accident: nothing a supervisor could have done would have prevented the accident.

Statutes vs. Court Judgments

The difference between statutes and court judgments was noted in the list of definitions, but this area might be expanded upon in order to provide a better understanding of the variations in the approach to legal immunity in the various states. A statute is a law which school districts are obligated to recognize. Ignoring such statutes is an illegal act and can result in strong action by the state against the school district. Such statutes are passed by state legislatures and become part of the state law. If a school persists in ignoring statutes there will often be prescribed penalties.

Court judgment, on the other hand, is a decision by a judge on a particular question which is not covered by a specific statute. Such decisions are often the result of a lag in the formulation of statutes to cover pressing problems. In many cases these court judgments set a precedent in the determination of future cases which are similar in nature.

In several instances court judgments have led to the enactment of statutes covering the particular area in question. It is entirely possible that the courts will reverse such judgments as situations change. In Arizona the courts have indicated that their original premise of holding state agencies immune from liability is no longer applicable as the result of a decision in the 1963 case of *Stone vs. the Arizona State Highway Commission.*[1] Although no legal action involving a school district has been brought to court it is entirely possible this opinion could remove the immunity of school districts if they were considered as a state agency. We find a similar situation in Illinois where the courts abolished the immunity of school districts as the result of a school bus injury in 1959[2] The same decision

[1] *Stone vs. Arizona State Highway Commission,* 381 P. 2nd 107, (Arizona, 1963).
[2] *Molitor vs. Kaneland Community Unity District,* 18, Illinois 2d 11, 163 N.E. 2d 89 at 96 (Illinois, 1959).

was recently indicated by the Minnesota Supreme Court.

In New York it was court judgment which eliminated tort immunity for school districts and the legislature enacted a "save harmless" statute in 1937 to protect their teachers. Thus court judgment resulted in the passage of a statute to protect the teachers.

Obviously, court judgments can be reversed either in higher courts or through a change of attitude by those sitting in judgment. A statute on the other hand cannot be changed unless it is repealed by legislative action, or can be proven to be in opposition to the State or Federal Constitution.

The courts have indicated in several instances that the immunity of the school districts may be the law of the state, but they do not necessarily have to agree with the law. In a case involving athletics a boy in Colorado sued the school district for injuries which he sustained during basketball practice. The court indicated the school district was immune under existing statutes in this state and that the responsibility for changing such laws lay with the legislature and not the courts. Despite denying the claim, several judges indicated that the tenet of immunity was obsolete as conditions exist today.[3]

There were two other legal actions, one in Florida and the other in Michigan, which attempted to set aside immunity as the injured parties had paid admission to attend an athletic event. In the Florida case the courts indicated the school retained its immunity despite the circumstances and any such change required legislation, not judicial decision.[4] In Michigan the court record clearly indicates the school is not liable for the negligence of its officers, agents or employees.[5]

---

[3] *Tesone vs. School District No. RE-2 in the County of Boulder,* 384 P. (2d) 82, (Colorado, 1963).

[4] *Buck, et. al. vs. McLean, et al.,* 115 So. (2d) 764, (Florida, 1959).

[5] *Richards vs. School District,* 348, Michigan 490, 83 N.W. 643, (1957).

2

Variation in State Statutes

IN THIS STUDY OF LEGALITY IT IS QUITE IMPOSSIBLE TO MAKE a blanket statement regarding the state laws which have an effect upon athletics. Many states have statutes which are similar in nature and yet there may be minor variations. Conversely, there are a large number of states which have statutes completely opposite in intent. There seems to be no set pattern although there has been a definite tendency toward standardization within recent years.

At the outset of public education in the United States the school districts were held as being immune from legal action. They were considered as being in the same vein as had been the King in European cultures, whereby developed the quote, "The King can do no wrong." This made him immune from legal action by his subjects. The school system was considered as an arm of the public and thus no individual had the right to sue himself. Likewise, an individual who was employed by a school system was carrying out his responsibilities under the direction of the public and this would tend to give him the right of immunity under a similar interpretation of common law.

Times changed, however, and this matter of immunity became more and more questionable. The attitudes of the courts were revised and several court cases have indicated that an individual in carrying out his responsibilities should be expected to do so in a manner which would not infringe upon the personal or property rights of others. In this way the individual employee could be held responsible for negligent acts which caused personal damage to those under his direction, namely the students. As a result, the teachers and other school employees were in danger of becoming the defendants in such cases. With this change in the legal viewpoint many states felt that school personnel should be protected from large financial losses if such litigations were based upon activities which were considered as within the scope of their responsibilities as an employee. This led to school districts being permitted or required, through legislation, to assume the cost and settlement of court cases which come under such a classification.

The final step in this legal transition has been a complete reversal of the original premise of immunity, thus making school districts responsible for negligent acts. The viewpoint is far from nationwide but it is definitely on the increase as state after state has been enacting legislation which places the full load of responsibility on the school district. The elimination of immunity has taken place in varying degrees and this will be further explained as we cover the individual states.

It is difficult to gain information on the statutes of the various states. A survey resulted in several conflicting interpretations and it was necessary in some instances to contact several sources. In only one book, *Tort Liability for Injuries to Pupils,* by Howard Leibee, was there a compilation of state statutes which could be applied to the athletic situation. Other information was supplied by State Athletic Associations, State Legal Divisions, State Education Departments, and a variety of references which included a limited number of examples of such legal information.

State Statutes

Alabama: The State Constitution forbids the naming of the state in a legal action and since schools are considered as a branch of the state government they share this immunity from litigations. There is a State Board of Adjustments for financial protection in the case of injuries resulting from negligence. Any claims made for such injuries must be made through this Commission and such claims are paid out of state appropriations made specifically for this eventuality. In no case, however, can such claims be made through court action.

Alaska: According to the Department of Education the school districts in this state can be named in a legal action as can the individual if negligence can be established. There is no "save harmless" provision. School districts can legally carry liability insurance.

Arizona: The courts have generally held that school districts cannot be held liable for negligent acts, but there is a distinct possibility that school districts will soon lose this immunity. In the previously mentioned case of *Stone vs. The Arizona State Highway Commission* the State Supreme Court indicated that the doctrine of governmental immunity would no longer apply in Arizona. This could affect any further cases involving school districts. Up to this point an individual could be held liable if it were proven he had been responsible for a negligent act. Most schools carry, voluntarily, liability insurance. They may also carry insurance to cover athletic injuries but the premiums may not be paid from tax money.

Arkansas: The State Constitution forbids the naming of the state in a legal action and the schools of the state share this immunity. It is legal for governmental units to carry liability insurance and this right may be applied to school districts. Such insurance can be used to protect employees named in litigations but the claim must be made against the insurance carrier and not the school. Recovery is limited to the extent of the policy.

California: In 1923 legislation was enacted which allowed school districts to be named in legal action for negligence by the unit, its officers or employees. In this state there is also a "safe place" statute which indicates that all school buildings, grounds and property must be safe from negligence. It would be possible to recover under this statute if the school districts had knowledge or were notified of a defect in these areas. Each school is required by law to carry liability insurance.

Colorado: The school district cannot be named in a legal suit, but the individual who may be responsible for a negligent act can be sued by the plaintiff. School districts can voluntarily carry liability insurance but the district does not waive immunity when it does so. The State Education Association provides liability coverage for its member teachers.

Connecticut: In this state a "save harmless" statute was put into effect in 1945. The school district must pay for the legal expenses of any teacher named in such a suit. The purpose behind this statute was not to remove the governmental immunity of the school districts, but rather to protect the teachers from financial losses. The law authorizes school districts to purchase liability insurance or to act as a self-insurer.

Delaware: School districts are immune from court action in negligence suits. There are no relative statutes and no court cases in this state. The individual responsible for the activity can be held liable. School districts are not authorized to purchase liability insurance with public money. The State Education Association provides liability insurance to protect its members.

Florida: School districts cannot be held liable, as their immunity was verified in a ruling by the Attorney General of this state. The premise is that a school is a nonentity and thus cannot be named in a legal suit. School districts may purchase liability insurance to protect employees in negligence suits but such claims are limited to $5000. The school district can also purchase insurance to protect students against medical expenses for injuries sustained in athletic activities.

Georgia: The immunity of state agencies is extended to school districts but a school district may carry accident insurance for bus transportation. The individual teacher can be named in a negligence suit.

Hawaii: In 1957 the Tort Liability Act waived governmental immunity for certain torts, including negligence. Interpretations have indicated that this act applied to school districts. These districts can voluntarily carry liability insurance.

Idaho: One source indicated the school districts were immune from liability claims. However, the Idaho High School Interscholastic Activities Association stated such districts could be held liable for injuries due to unsafe facilities while individuals could be held liable for their negligent acts. It was also indicated school districts could purchase liability insurance under permissive legislation. It would seem transportation liability insurance is mandatory. The respondent to a questionnaire supported his contention of school liability by citing the case of a student who was awarded $35,000 for a negligence suit in Caldwell. The State Education Association provides liability protection for its members.

Illinois: In 1959 the courts abolished tort immunity for school districts as the result of a school bus injury.[1] The State Legislature took no action to change the court decision but did set a maximum of $10,000 for each separate negligence claim. The State Constitution does forbid the

[1] *Molitor vs. Kaneland Community Unity District,* 18, Illinois 2d 11, 163 N.E. 2d 89 at 96 (Illinios, 1959).

naming of the state in a suit, but this immunity does not apply to school districts. These districts are authorized to carry liability insurance. Injured parties have one year in which to submit claims.

Indiana: The schools in this state are immune from tort claims. Individuals can be held liable. The school district can purchase liability insurance to protect its employees against claims which involve use of school vehicles. This has raised the question as to whether such action has removed school district immunity.

Iowa: Permissive legislation which allows governmental units to carry liability insurance may be applied to school districts, but this does not remove immunity. According to correspondence there have been no precedent-setting cases in this state. Individuals can be held liable and the State Education Association provides liability insurance for its members.

Kansas: School districts are immune from negligence claims. They can voluntarily carry liability insurance for transportation and the immunity is removed to the extent of the insurance coverage. Individuals can be held liable.

Kentucky: The school districts are immune and employees can be held liable for their negligent acts. It is permissible to purchase liability insurance for the negligence of drivers of school vehicles.

Louisiana: The school district is immune from liability suits, but individuals can be named in them. The school districts can carry athletic liability insurance but the cost of the premiums must be derived from athletic funds and not from school board funds. It is legal for school districts to purchase liability insurance to cover transportation.

Maine: Once again there were divergent opinions but the Department of Education positively indicated a school district could be held liable for negligence due to unsafe facilities, or for negligent acts leading to an injury. An individual responsible for a negligent act may also be held liable. The respondent indicated that both the school district and individuals may carry liability insurance, and added that they were strongly urged to do so, particularly coaches. The reply also indicated that no case against a school district had been successful but it was felt this policy could change. At the time of the correspondence a suit was in progress arising from an accident to a boy in a ski meet.

Maryland: The school districts share governmental immunity and cannot be sued for negligence. The individual can be named in a suit. The State Education Association provides protection for its members under a liability policy.

Massachusetts: A permissive "save harmless" statute was passed in 1959. The school district can assume responsibility for the acts of its employees if they are acting within the scope of their employment. The statute also authorizes the purchase of liability insurance by the school districts. The liability coverage, however, has specific limitations and a teacher involved is responsible for any claim beyond the limit. Transportation liability insurance is required.

Michigan: In this state the school districts are held immune from legal action. There have been recent cases in which the State Supreme Court has indicated that if it were not for existing legislation, which guarantees governmental immunity to schools, the court would have eliminated such immunity. The school districts, however, are liable for accidents involving school-owned vehicles due to negligent acts of the driver. The State Education Association provides protection for its members through a liability policy.

Minnesota: The State Supreme Court refused to recognize the immunity of school districts after 1963. It indicated that the immunity extended to governmental units would not apply to school districts as it had previously. The 1963 legislature, however, restored governmental immunity to school districts until January 1, 1968 as a defense in legal action but indicated that when a school district purchased liability insurance, which is permissible, the immunity would be removed to the extent of the coverage. Before January 1, 1968, the school districts were required to provide a "save harmless" provision to protect the teachers against financial loss. The State Education Association also provides liability protection for its members.

Mississippi: School districts are immune from court action, but the State Claims Commission will make payment on claims resulting from transportation injuries with a limit of $5000 for each individual case. The fund from which such money is awarded is collected from each school district which provides transportation. School districts may not purchase liability insurance of any type, as it is considered an illegal expenditure. Individuals are open to negligence suits.

Missouri: School districts are immune from negligence claims. The individual can be sued. There have been several suits but no teacher or coach has ever been held liable according to the response received.

Montana: The reply from Montana High School Association implied school districts were liable for negligence. However, another source indicated the school district was considered as immune. It would seem that a school district can voluntarily carry liability insurance. The reason for the discrepancy may be the lack of any legal action in this area. Members of the State Education Association are protected by a liability policy.

Nebraska: School districts are immune from legal action and there seem to be no precedent-setting court cases in this state. The purchase of liability insurance is not authorized by law.

Nevada: School districts are immune from legal action. They can carry liability insurance and are required to do so for pupil transportation. They can purchase accident insurance to cover athletic activities.

New Hampshire: School districts can voluntarily carry liability insurance to protect against claims in negligence suits but this is not considered a waiver of immunity.

New Jersey: In 1938 the legislature enacted a "save harmless" statute by which the school board must pay all legal expenses of a teacher named in a negligence suit. There is also a statute which will not allow the school district to utilize the "save harmless" clause when the case involves corporal punishment. The "save harmless" statute was not intended to eliminate governmental immunity but to protect the teachers from financial loss. The school district cannot be held liable for injury from the use of public buildings, grounds or structures. The school districts are also authorized to purchase liability insurance.

New Mexico: The school districts are immune but are permitted to purchase liability insurance to protect their employees. The purchase of such insurance does not waive immunity. Any claim in excess of the coverage is the responsibility of the teacher. Although school district liability insurance is not required most schools do carry it. The State Education Association protects its members with liability coverage.

New York: Court judgment indicated that school districts were not immune from liability and in 1937 a "save harmless" statute was enacted to protect teachers. In such cases of liability it is the school district which is sued and not the individual teacher. Liability insurance is a legal expenditure for school districts.

North Carolina: School districts are immune but can purchase liability insurance. Immunity is waived to the extent of the policy.

North Dakota: Governmental immunity applies to school districts. However, liability insurance provisions applying to governmental units may apply to school districts, but there is no waiver of immunity. There is no record of a successful suit.

Ohio: School districts are immune and it is illegal to carry general liability insurance. It is permissible to purchase such insurance for school transportation.

Oklahoma: A school district cannot be held liable. An individual can be held liable but there are no cases indicating a successful litigation. The school district can carry liability insurance for transportation but this is not considered a waiver of immunity.

Oregon: There was a variation of opinion but this can be explained by a variation in legislation. The school district does not seem to be liable and employees can be sued. The school districts may voluntarily carry liability insurance. In 1955 a *permissive* "save harmless" statute was instituted to leave the protection of the teacher up to the discretion of the school districts. It would be possible for a school district in this state to be liable for negligence if it were performing a proprietary function. A school district can be named as the defendant in a negligence suit when it purchases liability insurance and its immunity is removed to the extent of the policy coverage. Members of the Oregon Education Association are covered by a $25,000 tort liability policy.

Pennsylvania: School districts have been held immune in this state, but there has been a movement to remove this immunity through legislative action. The school district is authorized to purchase liability insurance to protect employees but there is no waiver of immunity.

Rhode Island: According to an interpretation by the Attorney General, school districts are immune. An individual or individuals responsible for negligence can be held liable.

South Carolina: The Legal Division indicated a school district cannot be held liable. Since a school district cannot be named in a legal action it was indicated there is no need for such insurance. It is legal to purchase insurance against transportation accidents but this does not remove immunity.

South Dakota: School districts are immune from legal action. The individual teachers can be held liable. According to Section 15.3815 of the Education Law it is permissible for the school boards to carry public liability insurance to protect employed personnel from liability suits if the negligence occurs while they are performing their duties as employees of the school district. This is another state which has a permissive "save harmless" statute. The State Education Association protects its members with a liability policy.

Tennessee: The school districts are immune from liability. The law does require liability insurance for transportation accidents and immunity is waived to the extent of the coverage.

Texas: A school district maintains its governmental immunity on the concept that it is a charitable institution for the public good. The purchase of liability insurance has been considered as unconstitutional. The State Education Association provides liability protection for its members.

Utah: School districts cannot be sued for negligence, but they can carry liability insurance. There are no precedent-setting judgments. Members of the State Education Association are protected by a liability policy.

Vermont: School districts are immune but it is permissible to purchase liability insurance and immunity is waived to the extent of the policy. Transportation liability insurance is mandatory. The State Educational Association provides liability protection for its members.

Virginia: The school district is immune but transportation liability insurance is permissible with immunity waived to the extent of the policy. The State Education Association provides liability protection for its members.

Washington: A statute dating back to 1895 allows for action to be instituted against school districts. However, there are several areas—including school-owned parks, playgrounds, field houses, athletic apparatus and appliances or manual training equipment—which cannot be the basis for any legal action. School districts are authorized to purchase liability insurance to protect their employees from such suits.

West Virginia: The State Constitution forbids the naming of the state in legal action. The courts have ruled that school districts are immune because they are performing a governmental function. School districts cannot purchase liability insurance as this would be considered an illegal expenditure. Membership in the State Education Association provides liability insurance.

Wisconsin: In 1959 court action abolished the tort immunity of school districts. In a judicial decree of July 15, 1962, a "safe place" statute was enacted but applied to only those buildings belonging to the school district. The school districts can voluntarily carry liability insurance. Transportation liability insurance is required.

Wyoming: In 1955 a permissive "save harmless" statute was approved and the school districts were permitted to assume the liability for the teachers' actions. Liability insurance can legally be carried by school districts and immunity is waived to the extent of the coverage. Transportation liability insurance is required.

Obviously the variations are quite numerous. New statutes and court judgments will keep this area in a state of fluctuation. As mentioned earlier the attitude toward school immunity is changing and the aforementioned statutes and court judgments make such changes obvious.

About one-half of the states hold school districts immune from legal action. In a few instances the school districts will assume the financial burden of negligent suits which name teachers as the defendants but indicate that this "save harmless" provision is to protect the teacher and does not remove school district immunity.

Several sources indicated there were no such cases and, therefore, there would be no legal precedents to follow in their states. There are several states where the school district is immune from such legal action and yet it is legal for these districts to carry liability insurance. This would seem to indicate there might be some question in future judgments as to the legality of this immunity and if this immunity were removed then the school district would be protected by liability insurance.

There is always the problem of determining whether an individual or the school district is responsible for a particular negligent situation, in which the blame could be directed at one particular individual, would eliminate the possibility of a legal suit against the school district. In those states where the school district was immune there could be no legal action if the district and not one particular individual was at fault.

In those states which have enacted "save harmless" statutes the school district is usually financially responsible for the negligent acts of its employees. Oddly enough there are states in which permissive "save harmless" statutes have been created in which the district does not have to assume the responsibility for the actions of its employees.

Individual teachers may carry liability insurance if they see fit to do so. This would be particularly important to those teachers who are employed in states where the individual is not protected by "save harmless" statutes or in those states where such statutes have particular restrictions. As a service to its members several State Education Associations provide liability protection through a blanket policy.

3

Supervision and Negligence

THE TERM SUPERVISION, IN ITS BROADEST SENSE, CAN BE DE-
fined as direction or management. In the eyes of the law,
however, the supervision of athletics must encompass much
more than this simple definition. All states require, in a
broad sense at least, that those individuals responsible for
such athletic activities be members of the faculty; but there
are situations where such regulations are being bypassed
through various devious methods. Such a practice has certain ethical considerations, but the information presented
here will be limited to the legal viewpoint.

Qualifications of a Supervisor

A competent supervisor for athletic activities should be
well trained. The courts have tended to approach the
coaching of athletics as a distinct phase of the educational
program, even though it may be classified as extracurricular, and concluded a person must be trained in proper
educational practices to be considered as a competent supervisor. Although there are individuals who lack such training and still prove to be competent coaches, they would
be considered the exception rather than the rule. However,
the courts cannot judge matters based upon such excep-
tions. There have been many instances where a trained

39

educator was far from the type of person capable of assuming the responsibility for such athletic activities, but then again this incompetence must be considered the exception rather than the rule. Individual judgment as to the qualifications of a competent supervisor for athletic activities may not be strictly comparable to that of the courts. If there is the least question as to such qualifications the court may take a dim view in negligence cases.

As an example of a court case in this area, a school district, in the person of one of its officers, assigned a janitor to supervise a gymnasium during a noon-hour program. While this individual was on duty a youngster was injured. The school district was held liable for negligence as the court considered such an individual as being without proper qualifications to assume such a responsibility. To quote from the court record:

> Restraining of young boys in grades in public schools in a gymnasium equipped for play and leaving them there to their own devices, subject only to control of one without training, skill or experience who makes no pretense of qualifications to duties assigned, is failure by the board of education to meet the requirements of the common law rule as well as statutory duty to establish rules for discipline in schools.[1]

It would be difficult to disagree with this judgment, as the individual responsible for the assignment of this janitor did not use common sense when doing so. This is not a reflection upon the ability or the character of the janitor, but he obviously would have neither the experience nor the training to cause him to be cognizant of the dangers that could exist in such a situation. In one school, due to a shortage of personnel, a janitor acted as a junior varsity basketball coach, while a bus driver was a junior varsity football

[1] *Garber vs. Central High School District, No. 1 of the Town of Sharon,* 251 App. Div. 214, 295 N.Y.S. 850 (New York, 1937).

coach. Their only qualifications were their experiences as high school athletes. This certainly would be fertile ground for legal action in the case of an athletic injury.

An injury which occurs to an individual while under the supervision of a student teacher may take on a different light in court action, dependent upon the viewpoint of the status of such an individual. At a recent conference of athletic directors in Albany, New York, Dr. John P. Jehu, who is the Director of the Division of Law in the New York State Education Department, was questioned on the exact status of the student teacher in his state. Dr. Jehu's reply was as follows:

> Cadet or student teachers now have been included under the coverage of the "save harmless" provisions (in New York), but on the other hand we still are in the position where the cadet teacher or student teacher is not able legally to handle a group of youngsters without the presence of the regular teacher. Now I realize that from the standpoint of teacher training this may be desirable, but as a matter of law it cannot be done, again you have your liability and your negligence question involved. If you have this cadet teacher in charge and an injury occurs, the plaintiff will scream to high heaven and undoubtedly will persuade the jury and the court, for that matter, that there was negligence in the selection of such a person as the sole person responsible for the class and therefore liability results. The cadet teacher is supposed to be there under the supervision of a certificated person. But as far as the liability is concerned they are also covered under the "save harmless" provision.[2]

This very situation arose when a student teacher was the only supervisor of an activity when a youngster was in-

---

[2] Report of the Statewide Conference for School District Directors of Health, Physical Education and Recreation, State Education Department Building, Nov. 15–16, 1962.

jured. The courts judged that a student teacher is not a competent supervisor for such physical activity unless under the observation of a certified teacher.[3]

Coaches will often have student teachers assigned to them in coaching the various sports. The aforementioned information clearly indicates it would be inadvisable to permit such individuals to assume full responsibility for an athletic activity. It would be more realistic to allow such a student teacher to assist, but always under the direct supervision of a qualified coach.

Foresight

There are times when a coach will experience unexpected situations which may demand his absence from the area where his group may be practicing. Oftentimes a boy may be injured to such a degree that the coach feels a need for immediate medical attention. If the coach is alone he may decide to take the boy to the doctor or to the hospital, indicating that one of the players should take charge during his absence. This can lead to serious reprecussions, as an adolescent boy is far from being a competent individual for supervising a practice session. From a legal viewpoint the coach must be positive that all activity will cease during his absence if he anticipates an early return, or he should dismiss the group completely if he feels his absence may be extended.

In the previously mentioned conference, Dr. Jehu was asked the following question:

"If I left the gymnasium and left a qualified student in charge, am I responsible if someone is injured?"

"The answer is 'yes' because there is no such thing as a qualified student. The qualification that the court

---

[3] *Gardner vs. State of New York*, 281 N.Y. 212.

will recognize normally is certification on the part of the person who is supervising."[4]

Similar circumstances resulted in one of the largest financial settlements on record involving a claim against a school district. A New Jersey teacher left the gymnasium to care for a boy who had suffered a rather serious rope burn. He informed the group remaining in the gymnasium to cease all activity during his absence. Despite his warning, one of the boys attempted a stunt over a horse from a springboard, fell and was injured to such a degree that he became a paraplegic. In the legal suit which followed the court felt the teacher had been negligent in leaving the gymnasium and the boy was awarded damages of $1¼ million. This decision would obviously be applicable to the athletic situation.[5]

What can the coach do to protect himself in the eyes of the law if he realizes that there are certain dangers present due to the nature of the activity? At the outset the coach must prepare participants to meet such situations in a way which will provide the greatest possible protection. Despite such preparation there will always be dangers inherent within the activity itself. The best coaching in the world will never eliminate injuries in certain bodily contact activities. However, the better prepared and conditioned athlete, will be less apt to incur such an injury than the athlete who is not so.

In certain situations the coach must use foresight in order to anticipate liability-creating situations. A person trained in this field should indicate a degree of foreseeability and eliminate dangerous conditions before they cause an injury. A case which set a precedent in this area of foreseeability was the tipping of a piano on a student, caus-

---

[4] Report of the Statewide Conference, *op. cit.*

[5] *Stanley Miller, et. al. vs. Board of Education of the Borough of Chatham,* N.J. Sup. Ct. L. Div., No. L—7241—63 (New Jersey, 1964).

ing a rather serious injury. The piano had been set on casters and was obviously unstable. The court considered it the responsibility of the supervisor in the area to foresee such a danger and the school district was held liable.[6]

Although the previous litigation did not involve an athletic activity the circumstances regarding the foreseeability of the situation could be applicable in a court of law. Assume that instead of a piano this were a loose backboard in a gymnasium and during basketball practice this backboard collapsed on one of the players. If the condition had obviously existed before the incident then the coach should have been able to foresee the existing danger and either rectified the situation or indicated that the players should remain away from this object until it was repaired.

In another similar case, which is more akin to the athletic situation, a supervisor failed to place a mat under a chinning bar. As a result, due to the lack of such protection, a child fell and was injured. The court also found this lack of foresight to be a negligent act.[7]

A school district in New York assigned two teachers to supervise a baseball game. During the game the spectators continually pushed forward, causing the benches to be moved close to the playing area. One of the supervisors stopped the game in two instances in an attempt to move the spectators back. One of the players, while going after a foul ball, tripped over a bench which had been moved forward by the spectators and was injured. This led to a negligence suit and the courts indicated the supervisor had been negligent in not foreseeing the danger and the school district was held liable.[8]

---

[6] *Kidwell vs. School District No. 300, Whitman County,* 335 P (2d) 805 (Washington, 1959).

[7] *Fein vs. Board of Education of New York City,* 111 N.E. (2d) 732 (New York, 1953).

[8] *Domino vs. Mercurio,* 234 N.Y.S. (2d) 1011 (New York, 1962).

A youngster was watching a baseball game and wandered too close to the playing area. He was struck in the face by a bat and the school district was named in a legal suit. The court considered the district negligent for not providing sufficient supervision to prevent such an accident.[9]

In the opposite vein, a student was struck by a bat swung by a teammate. In the legal action which followed the counsel for the plaintiff attempted to prove that proper supervision would have prevented this accident and therefore negligence did exist. The court indicated that such activities lend themselves to accidents which cannot be prevented no matter how supervision is provided.[10]

Assumption of Risk

The courts have recognized that certain athletic activities contain a degree of risk during participation. No matter what safety precautions may be taken, dangerous situations are bound to arise. In athletics we are assuming that the participants are doing so on a voluntary basis and they must assume the risk involved, if no negligence is present. There was a case in Georgia where a boy participated voluntarily in football and was injured. The contention in the legal action which followed was that this boy had an injury previous to football practice and he should not have been allowed to indulge in bodily contact activities. The court decided that this boy knew he would be participating in an activity which had an element of danger involved and, since he, but not necessarily the coach, knew of the injury, he had participated voluntarily. The case was dismissed.[11]

---

[9] *Germond vs. Board of Education of New York City,* 10 App. Div. 2d 139, 197 N.Y. Supp. 2d 548 (New York, 1960).
[10] *Underhill vs. Alameda Elementary School District,* 133 Cal., App. 24 P (2d) (California, 1933).
[11] *Hale vs. Davies,* 70 S.E. (2d) 923 (Georgia, 1952).

In this same area there is the situation of the coach warning the individual of the dangers in a particular activity. There was such a case which involved a physical education activity but which could set a precedent for a similar situation in athletics. A teacher instructed a class on the proper methods of performing a vault over a gymnasium horse. At the same time he indicated the dangers which existed and told the group they should only attempt to vault if they felt confident they could perform it successfully. One youngster, while attempting the vault, fell and broke his arm. In the legal action which followed the court found there was no negligence since the student had been warned and knew the risk he was assuming.[12] The same situation could very easily arise during the practice sessions of a gymnastic team.

The term "legal causation" will often enter into liability suits; this term implies that an individual created a situation whereby another individual could be injured. If such causation can be proven there is usually no question that negligence did exist. This matter of causation arose in a legal action in New York where a group of boys were practicing basketball in a school gymnasium. The coach was called from the gym during the activity and in the interim two boys collided and struck their heads. This resulted in legal action based on the premise that there had been no supervision at the time of the injury. The court considered that the accident would have occurred even if the supervisor had been present and his absence was not a causative factor in the accident.[13]

---

[12] *Sayers vs. Ranger,* 83 A. (2d) 775 (New Jersey, 1951).
[13] *Kaufman vs. City of New York,* 214 N.Y.S. (2d) 767 (New York, 1961).

Degree of Skill

In a legal action involving athletics it would be possible for the court to be determining the skills and activities which are appropriate at the various age levels. It is unfortunate that in certain situations a complete misunderstanding of the skills involved in athletic activities could result in a coach being held negligent. A lack of such information could result in judgment which, by professional standards, would be considered unfair. Who is to determine the advisability of teaching specific skills to athletes. In their book on school law, Drury and Ray made the following statement:

> There is a variety of cases that hold the physical education teacher or coach legally responsible for permitting children to engage in athletic activity that is beyond their skill, ability or physical fitness, or to participate in such an activity without proper preparation, training or instruction.[14]

As you will note in the following legal actions, the opinions expressed by the courts in this area of skills, ability, etc. may not be congruent with professional opinions.

Although the following three cases involve physical education activities, their close similarity to comparable athletic activities could well set a precedent in the area of athletics. A girl in California was performing a dive roll over two other girls. This has been a standard stunt in the area of tumbling for many years. The courts, however, decided that this was not a fit activity for an individual of the claimant's age and found the school district liable for requiring the stunt.[15]

---

[14] Drury, Robert and Ray, Kenneth. *Principles of School Law,* p. 72.
[15] *Bellman vs. San Francisco High School,* 11 California (2d) 576.

In a similar ruling in New York the school district was held liable for negligence when a child was injured doing a headstand. The judge considered such a stunt an unreasonable exercise.[16]

In the same state a judge considered it negligence when a youngster was required to do a somersault without having received adequate instruction.[17] This decision would seem to be reasonable.

These three cases could have a telling effect upon certain decisions which might arise out of the teaching of advanced skills which may be considered as standard by coaches. It could be that such situations could arise in the coaching of such sports as gymnastics or diving. Although the coach may be teaching a difficult movement to the entire group it may be adjudged that a fourteen-year-old freshman should not be expected to perform such movements as well as an eighteen-year-old senior. Athletic administrators realize that such a condition is undoubtedly true and this has led to the formulation of athletic groups for those more limited in experience, such as freshmen or junior varsity teams. In smaller schools, however, there may not be a sufficient enrollment to include provisions for younger boys and this could result in legal problems if the issue were brought to court.

There has been a tendency to extend the interscholastic program to the junior high level and sometimes even lower. In doing so the school districts may be creating a situation whereby there is an increase in the possibility for legal action. Since junior high boys lack the strength, coordination and experience of their high school counterparts, this must be taken into account. There does exist a degree of disagreement among professional educators in this area of junior high athletics. It would seem the answer lies in the

---

[16] *Gardner vs. State of New York* 281 N.Y. 212.
[17] *Clark vs. Board of Education,* 304 N.Y. 488, 109 N.E. 2d 73 (New York, 1952).

modification of the activity to make it more appropriate for the maturity of the participants. Such adjustments as shorter periods of play, changes in equipment to remove hazardous situations, elimination of certain danger-creating circumstances (such as the kickoff in football), and the modification of the facilities are all steps in the proper direction of protecting the youngster and, at the same time, protecting the supervisors and school districts from possible legal action.

Training and Conditioning

In the area of training and conditioning of team members there is often an obvious flouting of common sense and a failure to protect the health and safety of the athletes. Most states set specific dates when team practices may begin. In many such states these restrictions are actually a part of the education law and ignoring them could become a legal matter. There are coaches, however, who have organized practice sessions previous to the mandated date and if an injury did occur during such an illegal practice session the court would have no choice but indicate negligence.

As of this writing there is a legal suit in an Eastern state over the death of a high school football player. This boy was a member of a team which was taken to a "football camp" in another state and the practice sessions seemed to have gotten underway earlier than state regulations permitted. This boy died of heat exhaustion during an early practice session. The parents have brought suit against the school district and it will be interesting to observe the outcome as there a number of divergent factors which will have to be considered, particularly the illegal practice sessions.

Another outcome of such a malpractice may be that the coach involved, if he is teaching in a state which has a "save harmless" statute, may lose the protection of this statute since a school board would probably not include these illegal practice sessions within the scope of his responsibility. In the same vein we have the coach who indicates his athletes should be in top physical condition on the first day of practice, as they will be expected to participate in strenuous physical contact. This aspect will most frequently arise in football. The coach cannot assume the players will report in such condition and is obligated to prepare them for such physical contact. If a boy is injured under such conditions and it can be proven he was neither schooled in the required skills nor physically ready for such activity the coach could find himself or his school district involved in a legal action.

In most states inter-school scrimmages and games cannot be held until a specific number of days of practice have elapsed. In one case a coach lost his teaching certificate for ignoring this regulation. In another similar instance a high school football team was forced to cancel its schedule and forfeit all of its games. If there had been an injury during such illegal practices there is little doubt the courts would have felt negligence did exist.

Numbers of Participants and Areas

What is a reasonable number of students for which a supervisor should be expected to be held responsible? Decisions in this area have been rendered by the courts in dealing with physical education, playground supervision and the like. There is no case on record where such judgment has been concerned strictly with athletics, but it is an area where there might be some cause for legal action due to the nature of the activity. Assume that a football coach is assigned the responsibility of coaching a high school team without any assistance, as unfortunately often occurs. In order to make full use of his time he may divide the group into units, according to their particular positions. Obviously, he cannot be at several locations at one time. In an attempt to fulfill his responsibility of coaching the sport to the best of his ability he might well be leaving himself vulnerable to legal action in an injury occurred at a location where he was not in direct supervision and it could be proven his presence might have prevented the injury. This may sound unreasonable but it could occur. In sports such as basketball, wrestling or the like, where the practice activity is somewhat localized, there would be less chance for a negligence claim. In outdoor sports, however, such as football, baseball, or track, such a situation would be extremely plausible.

There are several cases in this area which, oddly enough, indicate extremely divergent opinions by the courts. In a California case it was judged that one teacher is *not* enough supervision for a playground with 150 children at play.[18] On the other hand there were two other decisions which indicated an entirely opposite viewpoint on the same situation. One court decision in New York indicated, in a very broad sense, that one or more supervisors for a playground was sufficient.[19] In another case in the same vein it was predicated that one supervisor for a playground with 200 children involved was sufficient.[20] A rather unusual decision, which was made in New York, indicated one lifeguard is sufficient supervision for an entire swimming pool.[21]

Obviously, these decisions are somewhat paradoxical. One indicated that a playground with 150 children re-

---

[18] *Charonnat vs. San Francisco Unified School District,* 133 P. (2d) 643 (California, 1943).
[19] *Graff vs. N.Y.C. Board of Education,* 283 N.Y. 24, 258 App. Div. 813, 15 N.Y. Supp. (2d) 941 (1939).
[20] *Purkis vs. Walthamstown Borough Council,* 151 Law Times Reports 30.
[21] *Curicio vs. City of New York,* 275 N.Y. 20. 9 N.E. (2d) 760 (1937).

quires more than one supervisor, while another indicates that one supervisor is sufficient for a playground of 200 children.

In another legal action the courts indicated there is no fixed standard when it comes to determining the number of students for which a supervisor should be responsible. It was clearly stated that the facts of the case are important and a reasonable approach must be concerned with the circumstances and not with any strict numerical ratio.[22]

In the case of athletics reasonable judgment would take into account the nature of the activity, the size of the facility involved and the danger inherent in the activity. The normal size group which could be properly supervised in most athletic activities, dependent upon the nature of the activity, by one individual should not be much more than 25 students. With more than this number it becomes extremely difficult to keep them all within proper supervisory observation.

In some situations in athletics the extent of the facilities available for large groups may create problems. With limited facilities there may be multiple use and any number beyond a reasonable amount may be considered as negligence. One court judgment considered a school district negligent when a gymnasium, which contained eight overlapping basketball courts, with a total measurement of 80 feet by 45 feet, was used simultaneously by 48 boys for basketball games. The court felt the school board, through its employees, should have recognized the danger which existed and which resulted in an injury to one of the participants.[23]

As mentioned previously, the particular situation and activity must be considered in arriving at a decision. Sev-

[22] *Rodriques vs. San Jose Unified School District,* 157 Cal. App. 2d 842, 322 P. 2d 70 (California, 1958).
[23] *Bauer vs. Board of Education of the City of New York,* 140 N.Y.S. (2d) 167 (New York, 1955).

eral handball games were underway at the same time in a gymnasium. A student was struck in the eye by a ball and a litigation followed. The court felt there was no negligence since the nature of the game was not inherently dangerous and although several games were underway at the same time this had not caused the injury.[24]

In this same vein, referring particularly to wrestling practice, Gallagher and Peery stated:

A dangerous situation exists whenever a coach attempts to handle a large number of students at one particular time in a limited area, and the potential exposure to injury becomes unacceptably large. One estimate is that each participant requires a space of approximately 50 square feet.[25]

Assigned Duties

In many instances it is difficult to determine what exactly are the assigned duties of a coach unless they are clearly defined in some manner; and generally, it is left to the coach's own discretion to determine the extent of his duties. In a court action the only reasonable approach in determining the normal procedure for coaching a particular activity would be to request the opinions of others who have had such a responsibility. Naturally there will be a variation in opinions even between these experienced individuals, but there will usually be some general pattern which could be used in determining standard procedures. Thus, an individual who varies his practices considerably from such standards might well find himself in legal difficulty.

Illegal procedures which have occurred and are taking

[24] *Wright vs. San Bernardino High School District*, 121 Cal. App. Bd. 342, 263 P. 2d 25 (California, 1953).
[25] Gallagher, E. C. and Peery, Rex. *Wrestling*. (rev. ed.), p. 80.

place at the present time were mentioned earlier. Practice sessions before the legal starting date, participating in a number of contests beyond the limits which are considered realistic, and other such procedures can result in legal action. A coach who permits such situations to exist may not only be breaking the rules of his local or State Athletic Association, but might well be ignoring legal statutes. The coach who has an athlete injured under such circumstances will be vulnerable to liability action and could expect no assistance from the school district since such action could not possibly be considered as a part of his assigned duties.

In some instances over the past few years there have been changes in statutes and regulations which have come about due to pressures created by coaching groups. In some states the number of contests allowed in specific sports has been increased. The previous limitations proved to be unrealistic and some coaches were bypassing these limitations by referring to certain contests as practice scrimmages. The illegal actions could have had some effect upon the changing of the regulations.

In some states the starting dates for practice sessions were specifically indicated. Once again some coaches felt this limitation was rather unrealistic and through rather devious means had their teams get an early start to guarantee that they would be in top physical shape for the start of the season. This was particularly so in football. As a result, several states have recognized the fact that the limited number of practice sessions may not have been enough to provide sufficient conditioning and agreed to allow an earlier starting date. In New York this has been done on an experimental basis and it was discovered that those schools who were allowed to start one week earlier, and practiced under specific restrictions, proved to have less injuries during the football season.

Although a number of coaches may believe that specific limitations are unrealistic they should not take it upon themselves to ignore such regulations. Concerted action to have such limitations repealed is the proper method of handling the situation; otherwise the individual involved could face possible legal action.

Although the various state regulations prohibit athletic teams from starting practice before a specific date, many coaches have developed a devious method of bypassing this regulation by indicating they will look favorably upon the players starting practice on their own prior to the official starting date. In some instances it is simply a suggestion by the coach, while in other cases the captains will assume the direction of practice sessions and may even take attendance. There are situations where coaches will issue equipment to be certain that these illegal practice sessions are run correctly and efficiently. Fields or courts are often provided and heavy equipment is placed in convenient locations. Although most coaches are wise enough to remain away from the area of such activity there are a few who locate themselves in the vicinity but do not actually take part in the program.

If an athlete were hurt in such a practice session and it could be proven that these sessions were encouraged by providing equipment and the use of facilities, it is questionable that the court would consider a coach or a school district completely free of responsibility.

This malpractice seems to occur most frequently in football as the students are not in school and it is easier to deviate from the rules since there may be less chance for observation, but as of recent years there has been a great increase in a number of other activities where clandestine practice sessions are taking place. An injury in any such situation might well result in a negligence suit.

Waiver Forms

In many schools each boy who participates in athletics is required to have his parents sign a waiver form. These forms are constructed in several ways but no matter what statements are made on such a form there is no possible way that parents can sign away the rights of a minor. If this waiver indicates the school district and/or coach will not be held responsible for any injuries incurred during participation, the form is completely illegal. The coach and the school district are responsible for guaranteeing that such activities will be conducted in a safe manner. The only possible value that can be derived from the signing of a form by the parents is to indicate to them the boy is participating in the athletic activity with their approval.

The following case, which involves more than the waiver form, clearly indicates of how little value parental approval may be. A sickly youngster was permitted to act as a store room monitor, where his responsibilities included the lifting of heavy objects. The boy indicated he had felt chest pains after such exertion but was permitted to continue working. After a short while it was discovered he had suffered heart damage, probably due to his store room work. The school district was found negligent even though the parents had consented to permit the boy to carry out these tasks. Obviously, parental approval is not a legal basis for permitting a youngster to engage in an activity which can result in physical harm, whether it be permanent or temporary.[26]

---

[26] *Feuerstein vs. Board of Education*, 202 N.Y. Supp. 2d 524 (1960). aff'd 13 App. Div. 2d 503, 214 N.Y. Supp. 2d 654 (1961).

Opinions of Others

There was a recent case in New York that will have an effect upon future decisions concerning athletic activities, although this case was more involved with physical education. A youngster was injured while receiving instruction on the trampoline. The instructor had utilized all of the proper teaching methods as described in a satisfactory teaching manual. This plus the fact that the instructor had spent a considerable amount of time on emphasizing the proper safety factors was verified by experts in the field, from both the high school and college levels. Despite his proper teaching and safety procedures the counsel for the plaintiff was able to prove the teaching of this activity was not included in the state syllabus. Unfortunately the reason for this was that the syllabus had not been revised for over thirty years and the trampoline was not in use in the schools at its original writing.

The important point in this particular case was the admission of expert opinion. In the eventuality of legal action it is possible that the defendant may require the support of others in his particular areas of specialization. If the coach happens to use methods of teaching which are either obsolete or differ radically from standard procedures, we may find the court tending to agree with the opinions of the experts. Departures from traditional methods are not necessarily legally questionable, but such variations should be based on sound principles.

The judgment of expert witnesses and the introduction of the syllabus led to the courts' finding a teacher negligent in another New York case. This involved an injury to a youngster participating in a line soccer game, when, during a melee between the two teams, she was kicked by another player. The syllabus indicated the game should include between 10 and 20 players and required an area of 30 to 40 feet. In this particular class there were over 40 youngsters participating in the activity in an area 50 by 60 feet. Witnesses familiar with the activity indicated the number of youngsters and the area utilized was a danger-producing situation. It was also brought out by witnesses that in order to participate in such an activity the participants should be well versed in various skills of soccer, which was proven not to be the case. The courts found for the plaintiff.[27]

How To Avoid Liability Suits

An athletic administrator who desires to indicate to the athletic staff the proper conduct to protect both themselves and the school district from legal action might well use the following list of procedures as indicated in the *Coaches Handbook,* as published by the American Association of Health, Physical Education and Recreation:[28]

A reasonably prudent and careful coach—
1. knows the health status of his players
2. requires medical approval for participation following serious injury or illness
3. performs services only in those areas in which he is fully qualified
4. performs the proper act in cases of injury
5. has medical personnel available at all contests and readily available during practice sessions
6. conducts activities in safe areas
7. does not diagnose injuries
8. makes certain that the protective equipment worn by his players is adequate in quality and fits properly
9. analyzes his coaching methods and procedures for the safety of his players

[27] *Keesee vs. Board of Education of City of New York,* 235 N.Y.S. (2d) 300 (New York, 1962).
[28] American Association of Health, Physical Education and Recreation. *Coaches Handbook,* p. 65.

10. assigns only qualified personnel to conduct and/or supervise activities
11. instructs adequately before permitting performance
12. keeps an accurate record of serious injuries and his ensuing acts
13. in all his actions or inactions, he asks himself, "What would the reasonably prudent and careful coach do under these circumstances?

Medical Aspects and Liability

INJURIES THAT DO NOT INVOLVE NEGLIGENCE ARE BOUND TO occur in athletics. Those involved in athletic supervision, whether as coaches or directors, must realize that there is the possibility that even though the injury itself might not be the result of negligence the action taken following the injury may result in a liability suit.

Physical Examinations

Prior to participating in athletics each boy should have a complete physical examination to determine if he is capable of standing the rigors of the particular activity. There have been several situations within the past few years where boys have suffered fatal injuries or have been disabled for long periods of time because certain physical defects were not reported. If such evidence was presented in a court action it is very possible that either the school district, the coach or even the doctor, if a physical examination had been administered, could be charged as being negligent.

There are various regulations regarding such physical examinations for athletes, and these vary considerably from state to state. In some states each athlete is required to have a complete physical examination before each sport in which he participates. In others the athletes are required but one physical examination for the entire year. These examinations may be the regular examinations that are administered to the general student body or they may be more complete in nature. In some situations the boy has the choice of receiving this examination from the school doctor, with the school assuming the cost, or he may have it performed by his own physician. If such examinations do reveal a physical defect which might be made more serious in nature due to athletic participation neither the coach nor the doctor should bow to pressures which would permit the boy to participate. In such a situation either of these individuals could be held for negligence in the case of an injury which was related to a defect which had been revealed.

There have been instances where the mandate requiring a physical examination before each season has been ignored. The athletes receive one physical examination as they report for their first sport of the school year and are not examined again, no matter in how many sports they may participate. A school district which functions in this manner is leaving itself vulnerable to legal action. In the case of *Bellman vs. San Francisco High School District* this was the basis for a negligence suit. This case involved a boy participating in athletic activities without a physical examination. The court stated that a boy participating in such activities should definitely have a physical examination prior to such participation. The court implied the coach should not require strenuous activities of any athlete until he is certain there is no physical defect which could be made more severe due to the nature of the activity.

Many medical men feel that one truly complete physical examination at the outset of the boy's participation each year would be much better than a casual one before each season. They might well be correct as they might often discover defects which could slip by in a more limited type of examination. Despite such opinions it is mandatory that athletic administrators strictly adhere to the state regulations regarding physical examinations.

There is an aspect concerned with athletic insurance which should be mentioned here, as it relates to the physical examination. There are particular defects and limiting factors which will result in a boy being considered as non-insurable. These factors will vary, dependent entirely upon the restrictions of the insuring agency. The following is an example of such limitations which would cause a boy to be non-insurable under the New York State High School Athletic Protection Plan:

Minimum Physical Examination standards to qualify for participation in interscholastic athletics:

Vision:

(a) If a contestant can see well enough to compete without endangering himself or others without wearing his glasses or lenses, this should be done. If it is necessary for the boy to wear glasses or lenses, the school physician must make the decision as to whether or not the boy is permitted to play. Suggested 20/100 minimum corrected with glasses, preferably shatterproof.

(b) One Eye—NOT INSURABLE FOR CONTACT ACTIVITIES

Discharging Ears: Not insurable if evident of active infection.

Blood Pressure: Suggested 135/85 maximum.

Heart:

(a) All heart murmurs to qualify only after cardiac study by heart specialist. The school physician must be supplied with transcript of electrocardiogram and copy of the findings of the cardiologist.

(b) Resting pulse rate—110 Maximum

(c) All suspected pathology should be further investigated.

Urinalysis: No more than a trace of albumin.

Pupils with heart disease, dislocating knee joints or hernia symptoms or tendencies will not be covered, nor

may they be insured against these conditions occurring in any subsequent coverage.
Not Insurable:
 (a) only one normal functioning kidney
 (b) only one normal functioning testicle
The School Physician is the final authority as to whether a student is physically able to participate.[1]

Despite these limitations there have been specific cases where boys who had the sight of only one eye were allowed to participate in contact activities. If any of these boys had been seriously injured and the insuring agency discovered they had been non-insurable under such restrictions the school district or its employees, or both, could be held liable.

There are certain conditions which may not be revealed in a regular physical examination and the courts have indicated that an individual supervising an athletic activity cannot be held liable for negligence if no other negligent factors are involved. This situation arose in California where a boy, unknown to anyone on the school staff, was suffering from a defect of the circulatory system in the area of the brain. The boy was struck on the head by a basketball and died as a result of this blow. The courts held there could be no liability since the coach had carried out his responsibilities as would have a normally prudent person and his actions had no relationship to the death of the boy. If there had been notification of the presence of such a defect it would have been the responsibility of the coach to protect the boy from the danger of a blow, but there had been no such notification.[2]

Another discussion of such disqualifying conditions was brought forth by Dr. James Russell in his report to the

---

[1] Form MD-1M-6-61, New York State High School Athletic Protection Plan, Inc., Schenectady, N.Y.
[2] *Kerby vs. Elk Grove High School District*, 36 P. (2nd) 431 (California).

National Federation of High School Athletic Associations annual meeting in 1962:

Conditions disqualifying a boy from competition are found. No attempt is made to cover all these conditions. Each case must be dealt with on its own merits but there are certain guides to decisions in these areas. Contact sports are football, basketball, wrestling, baseball and gymnastics. Non-contact sports include tennis, swimming, golf and track.

(1) MATURITY—By the junior year in high school, almost all boys have reached the same stage of maturation but some sophomores and freshmen do not reach full maturation and should be withheld from competition with boys who have. It is likewise important to spot the 8th grader who matures earlier than his classmates, in order to prevent him from injuring his classmates in pre-high-school activities.

(2) ABSENCE OR SEVERE DISEASE OF A PAIRED ORGAN—The absence or severe disease of an eye, ear, kidney, testicle or lung is an absolute contraindication for participation in contact sports.

(3) CARDIOVASCULAR DISEASE—The presence of a heart murmur is not in itself an indication to deny a youngster a chance to participate in sports. The murmur should be carefully evaluated and then determination made as to the boy's athletic future.

(4) ORTHOPEDIC CONDITIONS—numerous and technical—a medical problem.

(5) DISEASE OF THE NERVOUS SYSTEM—Need muscles to prevent injuries, anything weakening them, such as residuals of polio is disqualifying for contact.

(6) HEADACHES OR HISTORY OF HEAD INJURY—Any boy sustaining three or more periods of unconsciousness should be barred from contact sports. Some athletes have "glass heads." Approximately 50% of the deaths in athletics are due to brain injury and careful attention to concussions is essential.

Release from the Doctor

After an injury the coach must be certain the athlete has been released by the doctor. If the athlete states the doctor had indicated he could participate once again it is wise for the coach to verify this fact. It might be well to have a standard form signed by the doctor verifying that the boy may return to activity. If the athlete has not been released, is reinjured and serious complications arise, it could very well lead to legal action.

There was a case in the State of Washington several years ago which contained two factors leading to district liability. The school district maintained a football team under the direction of one of its teachers. This coach induced a boy to come out for football, a fact which was unknown to the parents. The boy was injured in practice and two weeks following this injury the coach supposedly coerced him into playing once again. The boy was reinjured and the father sued for negligence. The courts found the school district was liable as school districts are held responsible for the acts of its employees in this state.[3]

First Aid

The matter of emergency care for an injury occurring in athletics should be clearly understood by all members of the coaching staff. Generally, first aid is a matter of common sense, and yet it can become quite involved when approached from the legal angle. Where first aid ends and medical treatment begins is a moot question. To quote from the brochure put out by the New York State Department of Education that deals with first aid:

[3] *Morris vs. Union High School District,* 294 Pac. 998 (Washington, 1931).

School accidents and illnesses should be anticipated, and approved first aid services must be available at all times. Such procedures would give due consideration to the protection of life and to the prevention of unnecessary suffering and fear on the part of the child. First aid is treatment such as will protect the life and comfort of the child until authorized treatment is secured, and is limited to first treatment only, following which the child is to be placed under the care of his parents, upon whom rests the responsibility for subsequent treatment.[4]

First aid, in addition to being treatment which is temporary in nature, protects the individual from more serious injury and provides comfort; it is an obligation which must be performed. Some individuals feel they should do as little as possible in order to protect themselves from possible negligence, but such persons could be proven negligent if they did not take action to prevent further injury.

This particular situation was well described in the *Physical Education Newsletter:*

Another difficult decision which confronts the physical education teacher (and the coach) is when to administer first aid. In general you should not administer first aid unless the injury can be classified as an emergency and there is no doctor or nurse available. In such a situation you must administer first aid. If you fail to do so, you can be sued for negligence. When you administer first aid, confine your treatment to alleviating the emergency condition. When an injury which cannot be considered an emergency occurs, send for the school doctor or nurse and do not administer first aid.[5]

This matter of defining a state of emergency was brought

[4] *First Aid Care of School Emergencies,* The University of the State of New York, The State Education Department, Bureau of Health Service, 1962, p. 3.
[5] *Physical Education Newsletter,* Croft Educational Services, New London, Connecticut. Letter 15, Vol. 7, March 27, 1963, p. 4.

forth in a New Jersey case when a boy dislocated his shoulder in football practice. A coach, familiar with such an emergency, was able to snap the shoulder back into place, placed the boy's arm in a sling and sent him home. The parents instituted legal action indicating the coach should be considered as negligent for not having obtained immediate medical attention. The courts felt this condition would not be considered an emergency and the coach had no right to secure such medical aid without the consent of the parents.[6]

In another case which proved to be the reverse of the previous one, teachers detained a youngster after school to soak his infected hand in hot water. As a result the scalding water caused injury and disfigurement. The teachers were found to be negligent since the courts indicated if the infection was serious enough to require such treatment they should have called either the parents or the family physician.[7]

In another case a boy was hurt in a football game and the coach had the boy rest and returned him home two hours after the injury had occurred. The injury proved to be rather serious in nature with internal complications. In a suit which attempted to prove the teacher negligent, testimony by medical personnel indicated the teacher in no way could have known from the outward symptoms that the boy had internal injuries. Thus there was no negligence on the part of the coach.[8]

Thus the courts indicated that a coach cannot possibly determine internal injuries. In the previous case the coach's approach seemed quite reasonable to the court and the fact that no further injury was caused by the delay discounted the claim of negligence.

---

[6] *Duda vs. Gaines,* 79 A (2d) 695 (New Jersey, 1951).
[7] *Guerri vs. Tyson,* 24A. (2d) 468 (Pennsylvania, 1942).
[8] *Pirkle vs. Oakdale Union School District,* 253 P. (2d) 1 (California, 1953).

In a case mentioned in the preceding chapter, a teacher was sued for negligence when he had a boy, who had broken his arm when jumping over a side horse, walk to the school health officer, performed the first aid he thought necessary and had the boy taken to the hospital. One of the contentions made by the plaintiff was that the doctor should have been called to the school rather than having the boy make the trip to the hospital. The courts felt the teacher handled the problem in a proper manner and denied negligence.[9]

Not only is the administering of first aid an ethical procedure but it is a legal requirement as well. A supervisor is expected to protect an injured youngster from further harm by the proper administration of this important action. The lack of proper first procedures was the basis for a liability case in California in which a supervisor did not administer first aid to a youngster who had cut her arm severely. The injured individual eventually bled to death and the courts found that the teacher was negligent in not performing the proper first aid action.[10]

A coach is expected to perform first aid to the best of his ability and at the same time exhibit care in handling those individuals who may be injured. Careless handling or transportation can very well result in the coach being held for negligence. There are injuries in which it would be inadvisable to move the injured party due to the possibility of a more serious injury resulting from such movements. There have been several instances where athletic contests have been delayed indefinitely due to such injuries. Prudent coaches and game officials realize the safety of an injured player is much more important that the resumption of an athletic contest.

This matter of careful handling was dramatically em-

9 *Sayers vs. Ranger*, 83 A (2d) 775 (New Jersey, 1951).
10 *Orgando vs. Carquines Grammar School District*, 24 Cal. App. (2d) 567, 75 P (2d) 641 (California, 1938).

phasized in a case in California where a football player was seriously injured on the field. Although the coach suspected a neck injury he allowed the injured party to be carried from the field by eight boys. As a result of this careless act the boy became a paraplegic and the case was brought before the court with a claim of negligence. This careless transportation was considered as negligence and the plaintiff eventually awarded a settlement of close to $207,000. The paralyzing injury itself was not considered as being the result of negligence, but the movement of the player from the field in the manner described was considered to be negligent. Obviously the coach has more to consider than just first aid.[11]

Medical Assistance

The availability of medical assistance at athletic contests frequently creates problems. It is rather difficult in some areas to have a doctor present at all such contests. Most states do suggest such protection but find it difficult to mandate such a requirement. In smaller communities there may be only one physician available for all medical problems and it would be quite impossible for him to be at the football field when he is needed in the community for another type of emergency. Some states do suggest that if no doctor is readily available, then possibly the school nurse would be of considerable aid to the coach.

There seem to be no court cases which deal with this problem of medical personnel at athletic contests but this is no reason to feel that none will arise. If it can be proven a doctor was available for duty during the contest, but was not requested to be present, it could lead to possible legal action. It is possible that before long many states will be mandating the presence of a doctor, or at least the school

---

[11] *Welch vs. Dunsmuir Joint Union High School District,* 326 P. (2d) 633 (California, 1958).

nurse at athletic events. Most schools do have such individuals present at athletic activities, particularly bodily contact activities which would lead to a higher incidence of injuries, but a mandate would guarantee this.

Illegal Treatment

According to the definition of "first aid" it is quite obvious such treatment is to be considered only temporary in nature and the main objective is to eliminate the possibility of further injury to the athlete and to make him more comfortable. Coaches are not capable of either diagnosing or treating injuries and should avoid doing so. Even though an experienced coach may realize what is physically wrong and know the treatment which would be the best for such an injury, he should never overstep the limitations of first aid.

There are many coaches who infringe upon the area of medicine even though they may not realize it. Unfortunately such ignorance will be of little aid in the courts. From the booklet, *First Aid Care of School Emergencies*, mentioned earlier, we find the statement:

> Internal medication should not be administered even in emergencies to any child by the school personnel other than a physician who has seen and prescribed for that particular case. Neither should treatment of any physical condition such as sore muscles, sprains, etc. by any member of the school personnel be undertaken, as it might be construed as practice of medicine and would be in violation of the provisions of the Education Law, which prohibits such treatment. That would be true whether the method of treatment is massage or mechanical devices, such as heat lamps or whirlpool baths.[12]

---

[12] *First Aid Care of Emergencies, op. cit.,* p. 3.

Such a statement will undoubtedly result in a flurry of disagreement by coaches. Whether they are in agreement or not the courts must approach all legal actions on this basis. Obviously most coaches have utilized such methods in numerous cases, and due to their training and experience serious difficulties rarely arise; but they certainly cannot be ruled out as a possibility. It might easily be proven a coach had overstepped his bounds and there would be no choice for the court but to indicate the presence of negligence.

In the case mentioned earlier of *Guerriri vs. Tyson* in which two teachers placed a youngster's hand in boiling water because of an infected hand, the student suffered serious scalding and permanent disfigurement and the teachers were held to be negligent. As quoted from the court record:

> Defendants were not acting in an emergency. The defendants were not school nurses and neither of them had any medical training or experience. Whether treatment for the infected finger was necessary was a question for the boy's parents to decide.[13]

There have been some interesting discussions involving adhesive strapping for various parts of the body. One viewpoint is that all taping performed by other than medical personnel could be considered illegal, while another viewpoint indicates it is only common sense for a coach to protect his players from injury. There must be a differentiation between taping to prevent an injury and taping to protect an injury. In the first instance the coach who tapes or uses ankle wraps to protect his players from such things as twisted or sprained ankles and wrists can only be considered a prudent individual, if such taping is applied in such a way as not to lead to an injury. Conversely, a boy

---

[13] *Guerriri vs. Tyson, op. cit.*

with an injury should be under treatment by a doctor. The doctor may tape such an injury as a means of hastening recovery and preventing further injury. If an athlete is released by the doctor this would indicate he is ready for participation and a coach should be permitted to tape him as a protective measure in order to prevent the recurrence of this injury. In such a case this action should be considered as preventive in nature, not as treatment since a release would indicate recovery. A problem which does develop in this area, however, is where the coach, rather than sending an injured athlete to the doctor, tapes the injury himself. If the injury did turn out to be more serious than first construed this could leave the coach vulnerable to legal action. Diagnosis and treatment do not belong in the domain of the coaching staff.

Doctors' Legal Liability

Doctors are constantly aware of the legal aspects of their profession and in the treatment of athletic injuries they realize certain precautions are imperative. Although the doctor is held in a different light than the coach it is wise for the coach to understand the problems of the medical profession. Too often coaches complain about doctors who will not permit boys to participate although it would appear they are more than ready.

A most complete explanation of this problem was delivered by Dr. James Russell at the National Federation Annual Meeting in 1962. To quote from his speech on legal liabilities for the medical profession in treating athletic injuries:

> Most public spirited physicians who look after the high school team are unaware of their precarious legal position. Educational institutions and persons connected

with their sports programs are subject to legal liabilities, under certain circumstances, for injuries occurring during sports participation. Legally it makes no difference whether the doctor undertakes the care for a fee, honorarium, or out of the goodness of his heart. The usual charge is negligence.

Liability problems arising from injuries sustained in sports are contingent upon the same factors as those which are encountered in private practice. They are based upon the premise that there has been a failure to follow the standard procedures and established methods for treatment of an injury. The following can be causes of action:

1. Failure to recognize an injury.
2. Failure to prescribe physiotherapy or rehabilitation exercises.
3. Certification of a participant with limitation for a sport with strenuous physical demands and a high incidence of trauma—signed permission of the parents means nothing.
4. Permission granted an injured athlete to return to participation in the game in which he was hurt or even at a later date when his condition does not warrant such activity.
5. Premature termination of treatment.
6. Failure to follow up a case which is under treatment.
7. Failure to refer for consultations.
8. Failure to handle head injuries properly.
9. Promise of full, excellent, or good recovery and not getting it.
10. Unwarranted experimentation.
11. Failure to x-ray an area of trauma.
12. Failure to check a cast after its application.
13. Failure to re-x-ray a fracture or dislocation after the cast has been applied.
14. Failure to administer tetanus when reasonable or commonly indicated.

15. Failure to elicit an allergy history before administration or prescribing drugs. Allergy should be in history signed by parents.

Medical decisions made in the heat of a game are loaded with possible legal consequences. The following precautions should be taken:

1. Where the contestants are under 21, secure written consent of the parents for treatment of injuries.
2. Don't promise an injured player that he will play again by a certain date.
3. Check equipment carefully.
4. Disqualify an individual for participation in a sport if his physical condition warrants so—don't permit anybody to apply pressure.
5. A team physician should be covered by malpractice insurance either (1) institution policy or (2) individual policy.

From the standpoint of potential legal liability, the team physician is in a very vulnerable position. He must be fully cognizant of this fact and must perform his duties to the very best of his ability. He cannot become negligent in any area of his work without very likely becoming involved in the litigation trends of this day and age.[14]

Financial Responsibility

Unfortunately the public often assumes that once they send their youngsters off to school in the morning the school district is responsible for all ensuing incidents. This comes up most frequently in the case of an accident, in which the parents assume that since the situation arose in the school the district is therefore financially responsible. The only responsibility the school assumes is to provide a

---

[14] *Medical Aspects of Sports*, Dr. James Russell, New York State Journal of Health, Physcial Education and Recreation, Vol. 15, No. 3.

safe atmosphere for its students; but this does not eliminate the possibility of an injury.

This common parental misconception is extremely prevalent, as injuries do, of course, occur in athletics. In some instances boards of education have felt they were obligated to provide accident insurance. This is normally allowed through permissive legislation rather than mandate. Since school districts are supported by tax money from the public, pressures from the public will often cause the directing body to consider this expenditure a desirable one.

Legally, however, a school district is not obligated to carry such insurance, as was verified in a legal action in West Virginia. An individual was injured in school and was treated by a physician. This treatment extended over a long period of time and at its conclusion the physician submitted a bill to the board of education. This group refused to make such payment and a litigation followed. The court found the school board was not obligated to pay the bill. They held that public money could be expended to guarantee first aid treatment but not for any long-range treatment.[15]

Weight Control

During the past several years the questionable practice of weight control has developed in athletics. It occurs most frequently in the sport of wrestling as a boy attempts to lower his weight so he may compete in a class lower than his normal weight. This practice is not limited solely to wrestling but also occurs in other sports, such as football.

To achieve a loss of body weight there are several methods which may be utilized, including a restriction in diet and a loss of water content. These methods are

---

[15] *Jarrett vs. Goodall,* 168 S.E. 763 (West Virginia).

frowned upon by many groups. Blyth and Lovingood in their article dealing with crash dieting indicated the American Medical Association, the National Federation of High School Athletic Associations, school administrators, parents, trainers and the majority of coaches in the wrestling profession all condemn this practice.[16] With such evidence presented during a court action involving a physical defect or illness which may have resulted from such weight control, this practice could only be considered as a negligent act, assuming a coach directed the student to perform in such a manner.

There seem to be no legal cases on record but this is no indication that this situation will continue. In 1964 a football player in Ohio was considered as being overweight at the start of the season. He put on a rubber sweat suit over his football uniform in an attempt to lose this extra weight rapidly. The boy died from heat exhaustion since his body was unable to eliminate the heat built up in his body.[17]

Doctors Robert Murphy and William Ashe, both of Ohio State, in their report, *Sports and Climatic Conditions,* clearly stated, "There is no place for the rubber sweat suit in athletics as a means of losing real weight."

Blyth and Lovingood in their previously mentioned article presented three examples directly related to weight reduction which should provide information on the effects of crash dieting.

One of the most severe and disabling physical disturbances associated with crash dieting is acute pancreatitis. An outstanding example of this is a case study report by McDermott in the *New England Journal of Medicine.* A young man eighteen years of age returned

[16] Blyth, C. S. and Lovingood, R. W., "Harmful Effects of Crash Dieting." *Athletic Journal,* May, 1963, p. 30.
[17] Minutes of Proceedings, Joint Committee on Athletic Injuries of the Ohio State Medical Association and the Ohio High School Athletic Association.

to school after the Christmas holidays weighing 133 pounds. The aspiring wrestler wished to wrestle in the 123 pound class. After twelve days of severely restricting his fluid and food intake he weighed in at 123 pounds. Thirty minutes after excessive realimentation the young man was stricken with severe abdominal pains. Thirty hours later he was admitted to the hospital with a diagnosis of acute pancreatitis. This disorder required ten days of medical and hospital treatment.[18]

Another case involved a wrestler visiting the University of Oklahoma for a wrestling tournament. This visiting wrestler attempted to lose seventeen pounds in ten days in order to make the 115 pound weight classification. His diet during the period of severe weight loss consisted of black coffee and orange juice. He fainted prior to his match and was admitted to the hospital confused and semi-comatose. The diagnosis upon admittance was exhaustion and dehydration.[19]

A final example of what can happen as a result of crash dieting is demonstrated by a case study of a young boy taken from the files of the attending physician. A fourteen year old boy dieted severely for six weeks, dropping from 152 pounds to 126 pounds. Although he was urged to discontinue his fasting, he flatly refused to do so saying the coach wanted him down to 123 pounds. An analysis of the boy's diet by the hospital dietician revealed that he was subsisting on 800 cc of water and 490 calories per day, the diet recommended by his coach. The boy was hospitalized for two weeks and was completely incapacitated for two more weeks at his home. His diagnosis upon hospital admittance was related to kidney dysfunction.[20,21]

If any of these three situations had reached the courts

---

18 McDermott, W. V. Jr., M. K. Barlett and P. J. Culver, "Acute Pancreatitis After Prolonged Fast and Subsequent Surfeit." *New England Journal of Medicine*, 254: 379–380, February, 1955.
19 Robinson, D. F., Personal communications to the authors.
20 McGuigan, R. A., Personal communications with the authors.
21 Blyth, C. S. and Lovingood, R. W., *op. cit.*

and it could be proven that a coach had suggested such procedures, or even known of the attempted weight reduction, it is doubtful if the judgment could have been anything but negligence. Once again the important factor is—what would a person of ordinary prudence done in this situation? He obviously would not have suggested nor permitted such weight reduction.

It would be a simple matter for an attorney to support the contention that such a practice is improper by merely referring to one of the most familiar coaching publications. In the booklet, *What Research Tells the Coach About Wrestling,* published by the American Association of Health, Physical Education and Recreation, the authors clearly state, "Making weight is an undesirable practice for the adolescent." Who could question this?[22]

The Role of the Athletic Trainer

The term "athletic trainer" denotes an individual who has as his prime responsibility that of maintaining the physical condition of athletic teams. This would imply the guarantee that team members are conditioned in a proper manner to withstand the rigors of the particular sport, as well as proper care for injuries which might withhold the athlete from participating in the activity, or at least reduce his efficiency.

There are varying viewpoints on the value and the legality of athletic trainers at the high school level. In many states the schools are free to hire fulltime trainers, who may also have other responsibilities, but whose main task is to fulfill the responsibilities mentioned above. In other states it is not legal to hire an individual for this position. It would be possible in most states to assign this position of athletic trainer to a teacher as an extracurricular responsi-

---

[22] Rasch, Philip and Kroll, Walter. *What Research Tells the Coach About Wrestling.*

bility. Once again there are several opinions, both pro and con, on this matter.

Whether the individual concerned has been hired solely as a trainer or is a member of the faculty with this position considered as an extracurricular assignment, there are certain legal aspects which must be considered. In the eyes of the court this individual should never treat or diagnose unless he has had medical training. In some instances this individual may be a qualified physiotherapist but he must still be under the direction of a qualified medical person. The courts clearly indicate the scope of medical treatment must be limited to the medical profession and any treatment by an individual not so qualified could lead to a negligence suit if the outcome resulted in physical damage to the individual receiving such treatment.

In some states it would be perfectly legal for a trainer to treat an athlete if the method of treatment and equipment to be utilized were clearly designated by a physician. In other states it would be illegal for anyone but a physician to administer such treatment. A coach or the person classified as the trainer should verify the laws of his state in such a situation.

5

Equipment and Facilities

THE AREAS OF EQUIPMENT AND FACILITIES HAVE LED TO several legal actions which have been directly related to athletics and physical education activities. Proper and safe equipment and facilities are the responsibility of all those individuals associated with athletics, as is the proper upkeep and maintenance of such items.

Equipment

It is rare that one observes varsity teams decked out in anything but top grade equipment. Due to the positive attitude of athletic equipment manufacturers, they have, in order to guarantee satisfied customers, spent considerable time and money in research to produce only the best possible equipment. Coaches realize as well that they are obligated to protect their athletes. Most of them are truly concerned with the safety of the youngsters. Even the coach who is most concerned with the winning of games realizes an injured player is of little value in achieving this end.

It is therefore usually not at the varsity level where most legal problems involving equipment may arise, but rather at the lower levels such as junior varsity, freshman or even junior high athletics. In some instances these groups are the recipients of hand-me-down equipment which may be poorly fitting, unsanitary and badly in need of repair.

There is no doubt if legal action were instituted and it could be proven the equipment worn by an athlete did not provide him with the optimum of protection the court would obviously be inclined to feel that negligence might be indicated.

There was a case in Pennsylvania where the judge in a lower court strongly indicated his opinion of football. Since the school district had governmental immunity no claim could be settled, but if such immunity had not existed there could be little doubt as to this judge's opinion. This case involved *Martini vs. School District of Olyphant,* in which a boy was injured when he was sent into a football game with a defective headgear. The judge involved stated:

> There are many moments when a football game produces a commotion and violence which would make an Apache war dance seem like a Sunday School picnic in comparison. In one of these moments [the injured youth] lost his battered headgear and was stepped upon, kicked and otherwise manhandled to the extent that his nose was broken and he was carried off the field as if dead.

Due to the existing statutes, however, the court held football was educational and had to be considered a governmental function thus eliminating the possibility of liability.

Although there is no record of such a case, the relatively new mandatory regulation which requires football players to wear mouthpieces could create difficulties for the coach who is not extremely conscientious in checking this situation. There are boys who will avoid wearing this important protective device if at all possible. Since such protection is mandatory according to the high school football rules the coach is responsible for ascertaining that each boy is wearing a mouthpiece during all situations in which there is the slightest possibility of a tooth injury. It has been medically substantiated that the mouthpiece also aids in the prevention of concussions and other head injuries. Thus, if a boy receives this type of injury while not wearing his mouthpiece then a coach might well be held liable due to his negligence in not verifying that the boy had this protective device in proper position. In most legal actions already mentioned, and those which follow, the predisposing factors are usually the exception rather than the rule, and this matter of the missing mouthpiece will be the exception, but one which could result in legal action.

The following cases will indicate how court decisions often hinge on some minute factor. A youngster was struck by a bat which slipped out of the hands a player who was swinging at a ball. It was pointed out that the bat in question did not have a knob on the end, as do most bats, and was therefore a causative factor in the accident. As a result the school was found negligent for using equipment which could be considered as dangerous.[1]

During an indoor baseball drill a student was directed to hit a ball and run to a base in the gymnasium. Since the base was not anchored in any way the student fell and was injured. The court felt that such an arrangement was negligence and found the school district liable for the injury.[2]

Purchase of Equipment

There seem to be no legal actions involving the illegal use of school athletic equipment but coaches must be extremely careful about using such equipment for their own gain. There is no doubt that a coach who utilizes equipment which is purchased by the board of education for his own financial gain could find himself in an unpleasant predicament. This would most often occur in situations

[1] *Rapisardi vs. Board of Education of New York City,* 273 N.Y.S. 360.
[2] *Bard vs. Board of Education of New York City,* 140 N.Y. Supp. 2d 850 (New York, 1955).

where such an individual was involved in a profit-making venture such as a camp. There is no doubt such action could result in his dismissal as well as possibly to leading to legal action by the rightful owners of the equipment, namely the school district.

There was a situation in New York in 1966 involving the unauthorized use of school equipment by school employees which created quite a furor on the local level. A number of such items, including some construction equipment, was transported by school vehicles to privately owned property in a resort area some miles from the school district. Although it would appear no legal action was instituted this illegal act created a great deal of local criticism.

A second pitfall of which coaches must be extremely wary is the matter of collusion on the purchase of equipment. There are a number of situations where both unethical and illegal practices do exist. Ethically a coach should never accept a gift from a sporting goods dealer. This may not be considered as illegal but might imply that such a coach would feel obligated to the particular dealer. There have been rare incidents where sporting goods salesmen have offered a coach the opportunity of purchasing some personal items and then listing them as athletic equipment which is billed to the school. Both the dealer and the coach could find themselves embroiled in legal action if this situation were brought to light. Although such situations are extremely uncommon they could be the basis for legal action which could involve a coach.

In some states it is a legal requirement that the purchase of athletic equipment over a certain minimum amount must be let out to bid. In some situations a coach or director might wish to deal directly with a particular company—possibly due to a long standing friendship, faith in its service, or similar important factors. Despite the fact that the basis for such action might be well founded, the law makes specific statements controlling such purchases.

If these statutes are ignored an injured party, say another dealer, could well make things extremely uncomfortable for the purchaser, even to the extent of legal action.

These points are made to indicate to coaches there are a number of ways in which they may become involved in legal action through a lack of foresight on their part and are certainly not meant as a criticism of sporting goods dealers, who are almost wholly above reproach.

Equipment Finance

The legality of a school board's using tax money to purchase athletic equipment has been the source of several court actions. The laws concerning such expenditures will vary from state to state. In some it is specifically indicated in the educational law that public money can be used to purchase such equipment since athletics are considered a part of the educational program. The statutes in other states, however, specifically prohibit the use of public money for such purchases, and to do so would be the basis for legal action against the board of education or the individual who permitted such an expenditure. If the state law prohibits such action and a school does desire to purchase equipment or facilities, or repair and maintain such, the athletic program would have to be self supporting. In these situations the athletic program would have its own budget and the money involved is spent solely for expenses associated with athletics.

In several instances there has been a trend away from the separate athletic budget. Just recently, for example, in New York State it was mandated that all gate receipts must be placed in the general Fund of the board of education. It had been legal to use tax money to purchase athletic equipment but many schools still maintained a separate athletic fund. The Bureau of Finance and Control of the State Education Department recently indicated that all income for such activities must be considered as an income of the school board rather than being earmarked specifically for athletics. Hamilton and Mort, in their book, *The Law and Public Education,* stated the school board has the power and the responsibility to control the income from athletic events and this cannot be delegated to school employees, officials or students. A specific question regarding such income from school activities was brought before the courts in Pennsylvania. The district and county courts held that the proceeds from school activities belong to school districts and must be accounted for as are other district funds.[3]

The legality of the purchase of athletic equipment by a school board has been questioned in court action. In Montana this question was brought before the courts, probably as a test case. The courts indicated that such a purchase was legal.[4]

A similar question was raised in Pennsylvania as there was some doubt whether a school board had the authority to purchase such special items. There is a list of special items which school boards can legally purchase, but there was no mention of athletic equipment as such. The court interpreted the existing statutes as broad enough to include the purchase of such items. They also indicated that another statute which permitted school boards to use tax money to provide for gymnasiums and playgrounds was broad enough in scope to include the purchase of athletic equipment.[5]

On the other hand there was a rather unusual interpretation a number of years ago in Massachusetts involving the purchase of basketball uniforms with public money. In

---

[3] In re. German Township School Directors, 46 D & C 562 (Pennsylvania, 1942).

[4] *McNair vs. District No. 1 of Cascade County et. al.,* 87 Montana 423, 288 p. 188 (1930).

[5] *Galloway vs. School District of Borough of Prospect Park,* 331 Pa. 48, 200 A 99 (1938).

this state it was legal to purchase athletic equipment in this manner, but the question involved the purchase of special athletic equipment, namely the basketball uniforms. The law allows for the purchase of any equipment which is used on land under the control of the school board. This brought up the question of the use of such uniforms by the school team for away contests. The court decided that such items could not be considered under the broad term "supplies" and there could be no legal payment for these uniforms. Undoubtedly under present circumstances this precedent has been superseded.[6]

There was an interpretation of the State Law of Ohio in Opinion #635 by the Attorney General of that state regarding the legality of using school funds to purchase athletic equipment:

1. Boards of education are without power to expend public school funds under their control to support or promote the competitive playing of games by picked teams from the pupils of the public schools.

2. The authority granted by law to the Director of Education to prescribe or approve a course of physical education in the public schools does not authorize the inclusion within such courses of what is commonly termed interscholastic athletics or the competitive playing of athletic games by picked teams from the pupils of the several public schools.

3. Interscholastic athletics, as the term is commonly used, is not proper public school activity under law.

4. A board of education in Ohio is not authorized to pay from public funds under their control the expense of furnishing basketball, football or baseball uniforms for the high school basketball, football or baseball teams, as the case may be.

5. A board of education is not authorized to pay from public funds for the expense of transporting their basket-

---

[6] *Brine vs. City of Cambridge,* 265 Massachusetts 452, 164 N.E. 2nd 619 (1929).

ball, football or baseball teams to a distant point for the purpose of holding an athletic contest between that school and a team representing another school.

Facilities

During athletic events numerous accidents occur due to the nature of the facilities and such accidents might well result in legal action. Certain areas and activities will be more prone to the creation of such incidents because of the equipment and facilities required. In dealing with this area consideration must be given to all of the possible facilities which might be utilized for athletic events, including fields, gymnasiums, courts and even locker rooms.

There have been incidents where an existing hazard could have unquestionably resulted in legal action due to negligence. During a baseball game a first baseman was chasing a foul fly and was so intent upon catching the ball he failed to observe a guy wire which was supporting a telephone pole. He ran full force into the guy wire which caught him across the neck and felled him. There was no type of protective fence or padding about this wire to prevent such an accident. This condition had undoubtedly existed for a long period of time but no action had been taken to prevent such an accident. Fortunately the boy was not injured seriously, but if he had been there is always the question as to what the court's attitude would have been in an ensuing legal action. Situations do arise which cannot be prevented no matter how much supervision or what protective measures may be taken. In this particular case, however, this hazard had obviously existed for a long period of time and could have been rectified, if it had been noted as a potentially dangerous condition.

Although it did not involve an athletic activity there was a suit in California which had comparable circumstances. A young girl was playing in a school playground and was injured when she tripped over a cement box which projected up from the ground. The court found the school liable for negligence as this situation had existed for several years and they considered this sufficient grounds to consider that school had previous knowledge of the situation.[7]

Even though there was no question that negligence did exist, the courts in Minnesota found that a school performing a governmental function cannot be held liable. This case involved a football player who had unslaked lime enter his eye, which caused him to lose his sight. If this accident had occurred in another state where this immunity did not exist there would have been no doubt that negligence was present. As the result of similar incidents it is now illegal, according to the rules, to utilize this type of material to mark fields.[8]

Indoor areas can prove to be as replete with dangerous conditions as are outdoor areas. There are pieces of equipment and appliances which can lead to liability suits if it can be proven that some negligent act took place. In general, if an accident could have been prevented by careful safety inspection of the facilities or the equipment it would have to be considered negligence by the courts.

In one case a student was injured when he fell in the gymnasium due to a defective floor. A lower court indicated the plaintiff had no cause for action, but on appeal a higher court stated if the claim of a defective floor could be substantiated the school would be held liable. The contention was substantiated and the court found for the plaintiff on the basis that the school district was responsible for proper maintenance of its facilities.[9]

---

[7] *Bridge vs. Board of Education of City of Los Angeles*, 38 Pac. (2d) 199 (California).
[8] *Mokovich vs. Independent School District*, 177 Minnesota 466; 225 N.W. 292.
[9] *Katz vs. Board of Education of City of New York*, 162 App. Div. 132.

There was a similar case in Oregon but the school district was not held liable. In this case the suit concerned an injury suffered by a youngster when he collided with a radiator in a gymnasium. In this state the maintaining of a radiator in a gymnasium was considered as a part of the governmental function of the school and thus could not be considered as negligence, although it did result in an injury.[10]

In New York there was a case which involved the absence of mats on the gymnasium wall. A participant ran into an unprotected wall and was injured. The plaintiff contended that during an activity in which there is the possibility of a collision with a wall it should have protective covering. The courts indicated that protective covering on all walls of a gymnasium is not the usual practice and found the school was not negligent.[11]

There are several cases which involve the use of mats during certain activities. There was a question in one case regarding the use of mats against a wall which served as the finish of a foot race. In this case it was once again considered as not being the standard practice and the school was not held as being negligent.[12]

On the other hand there are conditions which may indicate that matting is necessary due to the circumstances. The use of a slippery balance beam on an oily floor without a protective mat was considered as a negligent act.[13]

Being familiar with or being notified of a dangerous situation which exists in athletic facilities or equipment will usually result in the courts deciding in favor of the plaintiff if an injury occurs as a result of such a defect. A boy was injured when using a defective springboard of

[10] *Spencer vs. School District No. 1,* Oregon, 254, Pac. 357.
[11] *Bradley vs. Board of Education of City of Oneonta,* 276 NYS 622; 243 A.D. 651 (New York).
[12] *Kattershinsky vs. Board of Education of New York City,* 212 NYS 424.
[13] *Bush vs. City of Norwalk,* 122 Conn. 426.

which the supervisor had been informed. Since the court felt that such information was in the hands of those responsible for the activity previous to the injury they were negligent in permitting the use of this piece of equipment.[14]

During athletic activities there will always be extensive use of the locker room and shower facilities. It is imperative that those in a supervisory capacity recognize that injuries sustained in these areas must be given consideration as they inspect the facilities for safety and the elimination of negligent situations.

Examination will often reveal many such facilities could be considered unsafe but all too often only the areas where athletic action takes place is inspected. There was a case in California where it was obvious the courts felt such prudence was imperative. A participant was seriously injured when a loosened locker attachment gave way. The courts judged that such a condition must have existed for a length of time in order for the accident to have occurred and it was the responsibility of those in charge of such facilities to guarantee their safety. Thus the school was found liable for the injury.[15]

Since the locker room can be a source of injuries, it would be wise for those in charge of an activity to provide some supervision in this area. However, it is not expected that a coach will have to remain in the locker room whenever it is occupied. This was the basis of a litigation in New York whereby the plaintiff contended there should be minute supervision whenever this area was in use. The courts indicated it should not be necessary for such constant supervision under normal circumstances.[16]

[14] *Kelly vs. New York City Board of Education,* 191 App. Div. 251 (New York).
[15] *Freund vs. Oakland Board of Education,* 82 P. (2d) 197, (California, 1938).
[16] *Donohue vs. Board of Education of Mt. Pleasant, N.Y.,* N.Y. Law Journal, Oct. 19, 1938, p. 1204.

Unattended Facilities

Although the attitude of the courts may at times appear as unusual, those in charge of athletic activities must keep abreast of such attitudes and do their utmost to protect the school district and themselves from possible legal action. An aspect which must be understood is that of the "attractive nuisance." By this term the courts have indicated it is the responsibility of those in supervisory capacities to eliminate as much as possible situations attractive to youngsters in which they might be injured. The classic case in this area had to do with two youngsters who climbed a fence about a railroad yard and were injured while playing on a roundtable. Even though the area was fenced the parents of youngsters were successful in a suit against the railroad as the courts adjudged the roundtable as an "attractive nuisance." It is not assumed youngsters are going to realize the dangers which exist in certain situations and cannot be held for their own thoughtless actions.

In New York we find the doctrine of an "attractive nuisance" has not been accepted by the courts as being applicable to every situation. In a recent litigation the courts decided that a school district was not expected to supervise playground facilities when school was not in session.[17]

In the same state, however, there is a case on record where a school district was found negligent because a teacher failed to lock a gymnasium door during an unsupervised period. A youngster wandered into the gym and was injured. The courts felt since the youngster was able to gain admittance to the gymnasium this had created an "attractive nuisance" and the teacher must be considered as being responsible for the injury.[18]

---

[17] *Streickler vs. New York*, 15 App. Div. 2d 927, 225 N.Y. Supp. 2d 602 (1962), rev'd 13 N.Y. 2d 716, 191 N.E. 2d 903 (1963).
[18] *Longo vs. New York City Board of Education*, 225, N.Y. 719.

6

Legal Aspects of Spectator Injuries

THE PRUDENT COACH AND ATHLETIC DIRECTOR ARE CON-
stantly on the lookout for situations which may cause injury to those participating in athletic activities, and might
possibly result in legal actions involving the school district,
its officers or employees. Unfortunately the safety of the
spectator is too often left to chance, and this careless approach has resulted in numerous legal actions.

Court decisions are difficult to predict because numerous
elements must be considered, including the immunity
factor, legal precedence, a slight variation in circumstances
which may cause legal precedence to be ignored, and public or proprietary functions. All of these will have an effect
upon legal decisions.

A young girl was watching a high school baseball game
while sitting on a fence 35 feet behind first base. The short-
stop on making a throw to first threw wildly and struck
the youngster in the eye, knocking her off the fence and
causing her to strike her head on the ground. As a result of
this injury, she lost the sight of one eye permanently and
suffered possible permanent brain injury. Her parents
brought suit against the school district for close to $80,000,
contending there had not been enough protection provided
to prevent such an accident. The plaintiff's lawyer implied
the girl should not be considered as having to assume any
risk while watching such a game, as it was supervised by

school authorities. The school board attempted to have the claim dismissed but the district judge refused to do so. The case was carried to the highest court in the state, where the decision was that any spectator assumes a certain amount of risk when he attends a contest of this type and found in favor of the school district.

This situation and the following, which is similar in nature, made it quite obvious to all concerned how unpleasant it can be when an unfortunate injury involves a spectator. There are several cases on record which seem to indicate that court decisions in this area will depend upon a variety of factors.

In a small New York community, a young woman was watching an amateur baseball game on the high school field. This game was being played by a community team, not a school team. The woman in question, who was sitting a good distance behind the backstop, was struck on the head by a foul ball and required hospital treatment. The community team had charged no admission and the school district had not charged this group for the use of the field. The attorney for the injured party attempted to prove the school board had been negligent in not providing a backstop of sufficient height to prevent such an accident. He contacted several schools in the area in an attempt to support his contention. Unfortunately, he discovered there was no standard regulation for backstops and the sizes of those in the area varied considerably. When all the facts were presented to the court the judge found no grounds for negligence.

There are court cases where immunity did not exist but in which the school districts were not held as being negligent. These court cases have done a great deal in setting precedents for similar legal actions. One action, which is closely akin to the preceding two, concerned the matter of protective screening at a baseball game. An individual sitting in the bleachers in the outfield at a baseball game

was struck by a ball. The plaintiff contended there should
have been protective screening in the area for the spectators. However, the court indicated that although there
were areas where it would be imperative to have such
screening, due to the location of the bleachers there was no
great danger in this area and thus no liability existed.[1]

Despite the fact that the law in Washington does not permit legal action for injuries incurred as the result of the
use of athletic apparatus, the courts felt this did not apply
to spectators. A spectator at a baseball game was struck by
a thrown ball and the courts found in his favor.[2]

The courts realize that there are certain situations over
which the supervisors of an athletic event have no control.
There was a case in California involving rowdyism where
a youngster was hit by a thrown bottle. The court decision
was based on the fact that those responsible for the activity
could not have foreseen the possibility of such an action
and could not be held responsible for the misconduct of
others.[3]

In New York State the school districts are not immune
in cases of negligence and an action was instituted against
a school district when a youngster, who was observing
a baseball game, was struck by a flying bat. The court found
that the supervisor certainly could not anticipate such an
occurrence and thus prevent it. The school district was
held as not being liable for this accident.[4]

The possibility of foreseeing a hazard, on the other hand,
can result in a successful lawsuit as was the case in California, where school districts are not held as being immune. A spectator was injured by a piece of glass in the
area of an athletic contest. The school was held liable since

[1] *Adonnino vs. Village of Mt. Morris*, 12 N.Y.S. 2nd 658.
[2] *Barnecut vs. Seattle School District No. 1*, 389 P. 2d 904.
[3] *Weldy vs. Oakland High School District of Alameda County*, 65
P. (2d) 851.
[4] *Cambereri vs. Board of Education of Albany*, 284 N.Y.S. 892.

it was considered the responsibility of its employees to verify that such areas are free from hazards.[5]

In a similar siutation, a spectator at a football game fell into an unlighted ramp on the school's parking lot and was seriously injured. The courts felt the school district was negligent in not placing a light near this hazard.[6]

Injuries to spectators may take many forms and some are more unusual than others. In Minnesota a spectator, who had paid admission, was standing about five feet from the sidelines rather than in the stands which had been provided. During the action of the football game two players rolled over the sideline and collided with the plaintiff. He contended that fencing should have been provided to prevent injury to spectators. The court indicated the purpose of such fencing was intended to keep the spectators back from the field of action, not necessarily to protect them from possible injury, and due to such circumstances the school was not held as being liable.[7]

Public or Proprietary Function

There is always the question of whether an activity is a public or proprietary function. This situation has and could have some effect upon future court decisions. A public function would be considered as one which a school would hold for the benefit of the public and particularly the student body. A proprietary function would be considered as one in which the school would have to be considered as in a profit-making undertaking. Although the school may charge admission for high school athletic events, these activities have been considered by the courts as coming under public functions since they are sponsored largely for the benefit of the student body. There were two

[5] *Brown vs. City of Oakland,* 124 P. (2d) 369.
[6] *Watson vs. School District,* 324, Mich. 1, 36 N.W. 2d 195.
[7] *Ingerson vs. Shattucks School,* Minnesota, 239 N.W. 667.

such court cases which attempted to prove that charging admission made a school athletic event a proprietary function. The courts, however, indicated such activities must still be considered as public functions.[8,9]

Conversely, there are situations whereby school districts could be considered as providing a proprietary function even though it might involve a high school athletic contest. In 1955, there was a case in Arizona where a school district was held liable for the injury to a spectator as the result of a fall through a broken railing. In this instance, the school district had leased its stadium to another school for a fee and as a result the activity became proprietary since it was not an athletic contest for its own student body. Thus, it had entered into a profit-making enterprise and could be held liable.[10]

Oddly enough there was another similar court action in Virginia where the judgment was somewhat contrary. The activity involved was not athletic in nature but had so many similar aspects that it does bear mentioning. A school board leased its auditorium to a group from outside the school for a concert. A spectator slipped on a waxed floor and sued the board, contending this was a proprietary function. The courts felt, however, that although the auditorium had been leased the nature of the activity, a concert, was for the improvement of the culture of both the students and the community and did not consider the activity as being proprietary. Therefore, there was no cause for holding the school liable.[11]

---

[8] *Thompson vs. Board of Education,* City of Millville, 79 A (2nd) 100 (New Jersey).
[9] *Reed vs. Rhead County,* 225 S.W. (2nd) 49 (Tennessee).
[10] *Sawaya vs. Tucson High School District No. 1,* 281 P. (2d) 105 (Arizona).
[11] *Kellam vs. School Board of City of Norfolk,* 202 Va. 252, 117 S.E. 2d 96.

Bleachers and Stands

The construction of bleachers and stands has led to several court actions with varying outcomes dependent upon circumstances and existing statutes. Temporary bleachers were constructed in a school for a special athletic event and when they collapsed resulted in several injuries. The school district, however, could not be sued for negligence due to its immunity (in the State of Iowa).[12]

A court in Michigan handed down a similar decision in an action brought about due to the collapse of bleachers during a football game. They applied the doctrine of immunity, indicating athletics were to be considered as a phase of the overall education program and the game was, therefore, a governmental function.[13]

There was a similar legal action when a poorly constructed bleacher collapsed at an athletic event at the University of Minnesota. Despite the fact that there was negligence in such construction, the athletic association, which was named as the defendant, was considered as a part of the university and since this institution was part of the state educational system it was immune from such negligence suits.[14]

The exact opposite decision was arrived at in Michigan as the courts judged the athletic association did not represent the educational institution but rather the students and the officers of the organization itself. Stands constructed by this athletic association at the University of Michigan collapsed and the plaintiff was injured. Due to the interpretation of the relationship of the association to

[12] *Larsen vs. Independent School District of Kane*, 223 Iowa 691.

[13] *Richards vs. School District of Birmingham*, 348 Mich. 490, 83 N.W. 2d 643.

[14] *George vs. University of Minnesota Athletic Association*, 107 Minn. 424.

the university, it was held as being negligent in the construction of such stands.[15]

The state of Washington holds that a school district is immune from legal action for injuries which occur during the use of athletic apparatus or manual training equipment. A spectator was injured at a football game when a railing on the bleachers gave way. The school district contended that under these circumstances it should be immune. The court, on the other hand, indicated that a railing on a bleacher cannot be considered as coming under the immunity regulations, and if it was negligent in this situation, the school should be held liable.[16]

Attendance at Athletic Contests

The courts have also clearly indicated that it is within the domain of athletic supervisors to determine who shall attend school functions. In order to guarantee safety and proper conduct at athletic events, those responsible for such activities may eject any spectators and refund their admission to protect the other spectators. Likewise, they may refuse admission to any individual for the same reasons. Legal opinion indicates the school has no obligation to admit or allow to remain any individual who may cause unpleasant or unsafe situations to develop.

This opinion was clearly stated by Hamilton and Mort in their book on school law:

It has been held that spectators at an athletic or other school function are only licensees and may be ejected from the exhibition upon return of the admission fee. By the same token, the school authorities may refuse admission to any person for any reason or no reason at all. In

---

[15] *Scott vs. University of Michigan Athletic Association,* 152 Michigan 664; 116 N.W. 624.
[16] *Juntilla vs. Everett School District No. 24,* Washington; 35 Pac. (2nd) 78.

other words, there is no legal obligation upon the authorities to admit any person to school functions, or to permit him to remain after he has been admitted.[17]

Obviously, there have been numerous legal actions which have involved injuries to spectators. The court decisions, of course, will be determined by the prevailing statutes of the state. Even though school districts may be immune from liability suits, if the responsibility for the negligent act can be attributed to an individual, then he might well become involved in the litigation. Spectator safety must be one of the first considerations of the director of athletics. Too often considerations are limited to the participants and supervisors could leave themselves vulnerable for such legal action in overlooking the possibility of situations dangerous to spectators.

Most states have included in their legal statutes specific regulations which are intended to protect any individual who may utilize school facilities. The laws must be considered as being applicable to the spectators at athletic events. As an example, in New York State these laws appear in the Education Law, Article XX, Section 167:

1. Doors must swing out and have anti-panic bars.
2. Exit signs must be illuminated.
3. There should be no assembly area above the first floor in wooden buildings.
4. Exits must never be locked.
5. There must be grills over all glass doors that may be used as exits.

---

[17] Hamilton, Robert and Mort, Paul, *The Law and Public Education,* p. 127.

7

The Legal Aspects of Transportation

LEGAL ATTITUDES TOWARD ACCIDENTS INVOLVING SCHOOL transportation differ considerably from those generally indicated toward other types of school accidents. This is undoubtedly due to the general feeling that the transportation of students involves a greater incidence of hazardous situations. As noted previously, there is a distinct variation in various state statutes where school transportation is involved. The school districts in several states, which are immune from most legal action, find this immunity may not hold true for transportation accidents. Some states make it illegal to purchase liability insurance except for transportation protection. There are also states which have special funds set aside for just such incidents. Obviously, there is more apprehension over transportation accidents than there is over accidents in other areas of the school program. Investigation would seem to indicate school districts feel more responsible for such incidents since it is mandated that youngsters attend school and with the combining of school districts for more efficient units it becomes a requisite that many youngsters must ride school buses.

The court records are replete with litigations involving school transportation but a few examples which would be applicable to the transportation of athletic groups should suffice. Some of these actions are directly related to athletic team transportation, while others could be used as precedent setting in similar situations.

100

The Use of Public Funds for Athletic Transportation

It appears as though the present attitude toward athletic team transportation is much more liberal than it was in previous years. With the concept that athletics should be considered as an integral part of the educational development of the student then it should be considered legal to expend public funds for the transportation of such groups so they may participate in this educational activity, whether it be called curricular, extracurricular or recreational.

Mort and Hamilton in their book, *The Law and Public Education,* indicated it was their feeling, as a result of extensive investigation, that school funds could be used on transportation for educational purposes if express legislative authority is granted. This would seem to indicate that as an educational activity public money could be spent for the transportation of athletic teams.

There have been a number of legal interpretations, statutes and even legal actions which have involved this matter of transportation for athletic groups. One such legal action was brought before the Supreme Court of Iowa a number of years ago. Their decision indicated school districts could provide transportation for certain pupils to and from school, but they had no right to transport pupils to basketball games.[1]

The Supreme Court of Utah was faced with a similar case and its decision differed somewhat. It agreed in part with the Iowa decision but indicated transportation should be permitted if the students' presence was required after school hours. A broad interpretation of this decision would therefore permit the transportation of athletic teams through the use of public funds.[2]

[1] *Schmidt vs. Blair,* 203 Iowa 1016, 213 N.W. 593 (1927).
[2] *Bear vs. Board of Education of No. Summit School District, et. al.,* 81 Utah 51, 16 P 2d 900 (1932).

In South Dakota there is a statute which clearly indicates transportation can be provided for interschool athletic competition and other educational activities if the board of education approves. Minnesota has a law which is broader than that in South Dakota as it states that transportation is authorized for curricular, extracurricular and recreational activities.

Foresight In Transportation

In the pamphlet "The Physical Education Instructor and Safety" there is specific list of safety precautions the supervisor should take into account when arranging for athletic team transportation:

1. Students should be allowed to travel in only bonded common carriers or school owned buses.
2. If students are allowed to travel in private cars, the school administrator should adhere to the liability law requirements of his state.
3. Students should not be allowed to transport athletic teams unless they are authorized drivers of school buses. The use of students to drive private cars used to tranpsort athletic teams is considered undesirable from liability and other angles.[3]

If the school does use bonded common carriers it is the responsibility of those making such arrangements to ascertain the vehicles to be utilized are safe. At the present time most states have strict regulations regarding the inspection of vehicles which are to be used for public transportation, but there are situations where, for the sake of a few dollars, a school might not be too particular in its choice. If an accident did occur while using a vehicle which might be considered as not safe, the school district, or the person

[3] "The Physical Education Instructor and Safety," High School Series, Bulletin No. 2, National Education Association (1948), p. 36.

responsible for obtaining such transportation, might well be held as being negligent. In those states which do hold that districts are immune from liability action, the transportation company or even the driver himself might well be held for negligence.

The school employee involved in the hiring of such carriers would find it advisable to check on the type of insurance and the limits of such insurance as carried by the transportation company. In the event of an accident proper coverage could well save either the school district or the individuals involved large financial losses.

An undesirable situation is that of the coach driving a school vehicle to athletic contests. This may be standard practice in some areas but there has been a definite decrease in this procedure over the past several years. If an accident did occur and the coach was called upon to testify, it might be proven that he did not have the necessary experience in handling large vehicles for the law to consider him as being competent. The courts could easily indicate that coaching and driving a bus are in no way related and it would not be in the best interests of safety to have such an individual responsible for transporting athletic teams. This could possibly lead to either the coach or the school district's being held negligent.

Court Decisions on Negligence Claims

There are innumerable court cases which have involved school transportation, but a few examples should indicate the attitudes which have been most frequently exhibited by the courts and, at the same time, denote cases which might be precedent-setting in nature.

There was an unusual situation which arose in Maryland regarding the violation of a particular statute. The courts found a school could not claim immunity if an accident occurred in which there was a definite violation of an existing statute. In this particular situation a school bus did not contain a safety lock as was required by state law. As a result, a child fell from the bus and was killed. Due to the violation of this statute it was considered as a proximate cause of the accident and, therefore, the school district lost the protection of immunity.[4]

There have been several cases in which the courts have indicated the driver of a school bus must exhibit the highest degree of care since his passengers are youngsters and may not be cognizant of the existing dangers. As mentioned earlier, in order to fulfill the school attendance regulations it may be necessary for youngsters to travel by bus and it is the responsibility of the school district and particularly school bus drivers to guarantee the safety of the students. If there is any question as to the prudence of the school bus driver the courts have specified the school or its employees, depending upon the immunity provision, will be held liable.[5,6,7]

The transportation of athletic teams or spectators to athletic activities will oftentimes result in the overloading of buses. In the transporting of teams it is not only the team personnel but the matter of equipment which may result in overloading. With spectators it may be a lack of properly anticipating the number of students who desire to attend the contest. In either case, if it can be proven the bus was overloaded there is no doubt the school district or its employees could be held for negligence in the case of an accident. This was the attitude of the court in a transportation accident in New York which involved an overloaded bus.[8]

There was an incident in New Hampshire which directly

[4] *Parr vs. Board of County Commissioners,* 207 Md. 91, 113 A. 2d 397 (1955).

[5] *Phillips vs. Hardgrove,* 161 Washington 121, 296 P. 559 (1931).

[6] *Davidson vs. Horne,* 71 S.E. (2d) 464 (Georgia, 1952).

[7] *Van Cleave vs. Illini Coach Co.,* N.E. (2d) 398 (Illinois, 1951).

[8] *People vs. Case,* 33 N.Y.S. (2d) 1, 263 App. Div. 342 (1942).

involved the transportation of athletes following a practice session. It was the usual procedure in this school to transport the athletes from the field to the school by truck, immediately after practice. The coach would supervise the loading of the truck and blow a whistle when the truck was loaded and ready to leave. In this instance the driver of the truck proceeded to have the boys climb onto the truck without the coach being present to supervise the loading. The driver assumed all of the boys were on the truck and started to move. At that moment one of the boys was climbing onto the truck by putting his foot on a rear tire to reach the truck bed. When the truck started to move he fell under the rear wheels and was severely injured. In the court action which followed, the defense counsel implied the boy should have known the danger and had contributed to the negligent act. The court felt the boy did not know the wheel would start to roll as he attempted to get aboard and the driver should be held liable for the negligent act.[9]

In Georgia a negligence decision was based on imprudent speed. The bus, which was traveling over the legal speed limit, skidded and a youngster was thrown from the vehicle and was killed. The courts indicated the imprudent speed was a cause for negligence.[10]

There were two cases which involved situations beyond the control of the driver and in both instances the courts held a student injured or killed on a school bus due to his own negligence or an act of God was beyond the control of the driver. The driver should exhibit constant care to insure the safety of students but he cannot be expected to watch each one.[11,12]

Under somewhat similar circumstances the school or its employees may be held negligent if there has been a com-

[9] *Beardsell vs. Tilton School,* 200 A 783 (New Hampshire, 1938).

[10] *Roberts vs. Baker,* 192 S.E. 104 (Georgia, 1938).

[11] *Lewis vs. Halbert,* 67 S.W. (2d) 430 (Texas, 1933).

[12] *Harrison vs. McVeigh,* 5 S.E. (2d) 76 (Georgia, 1939).

plaint regarding certain existing dangers. In one such case there had been several complaints regarding mischievous conduct by certain children. As a result of this mischief a youngster was injured and the plaintiff contended the accident could have been prevented. The courts indicated the complaints constituted a warning; the driver should have taken preventive measures and his lack of doing so constituted a negligent act on his part.[13]

In most cases where the school district is exempt from tort liability this immunity is applied to bus accidents. There was a school bus accident in Virginia where a youngster was killed. The courts held the school district was immune but found the individual driving the bus could be held liable if his actions proved to be negligent.[14]

Although there are several cases on record where individuals were held negligent, there was a case in Iowa in which the courts did not follow this precedent. In a litigation involving a school bus accident the courts indicated the bus driver was performing a governmental function and therefore had the protection of immunity.[15]

There have been court cases which questioned the capability of the driver of a bus that had been involved in an accident. A North Carolina case involved the proficiency of a bus driver who lost control of a bus while transporting school children and resulted in the death of one of the youngsters. The school board was named as the defendant by the parents of the youngster. The courts pointed out the school board could only be considered liable if it hired bus drivers in a non-prudent manner and since this was not the case the school board could not be held liable.[16]

There were two similar situations in Georgia where the

---

[13] *Garrett vs. Bee Line Inc.,* 13 N.Y.S. (2d) 154 (New York, 1939).
[14] *Wynn vs. Gaudy,* 197, S.E. 527 (Virginia, 1938).
[15] *Hibbs vs. Independent School District of Green Mountain,* 218 Iowa 841, 251, N.W. 606 (1933).
[16] *Betts vs. Jones et al.* 166 S.E. 589 (No. Carolina).

school districts were considered immune. These litigations questioned the qualifications for school bus drivers, as they are hired by school districts. The courts arrived at a similar decision to the one in the previous case and even noted it was not negligence if the school board happened to hire poorly qualified personnel except if the board knew of the poor quality of the individual so hired.[17,18]

There was an incident in New York State a few years ago which had an extremely telling effect upon a particular school district. A group of youngsters were on their way to a music festival in a school-owned station wagon driven by one of the teachers. The vehicle was involved in a fatal accident and all the passengers, including the teacher, were killed. Although the actual cause of the accident was never specified, in the ensuing litigation brought by the parents, the court felt the driver of the vehicle had been negligent and could be held liable for the accident. Since there is a "save harmless" clause in New York the school was held responsible for the actions of its employee. The school district carried liability insurance for such accidents but due to the magnitude of the claims these even exceeded the amount of insurance coverage. The school district, in order to make restitution for this horrible tragedy, found it necessary to increase the tax rate of the district an enormous amount for several years.

Although only one of these cases directly involved the transportation of athletic groups the decisions would most certainly apply to such transportation. The transportation of school age youngsters would be viewed from a similar viewpoint, whether it be to or from school, or a trip for an athletic activity. There are a number of other cases but they are quite similar in nature and the court decisions were comparable.

[17] *Roberts vs. Baker,* 57 Ga. 733, 196 S.E. 104 (1938).
[18] *Krasner vs. Harper,* 90 Ga. App. 128, 82 S.E. 2d 267 (1954).

Privately Owned Vehicles

The situation of transporting school-aged youngsters in privately owned vehicles is more apt to occur in those activities which we consider extracurricular. Music, athletics and other such activities are of a nature whereby small groups of students may be transported in private cars, either for participation in such activities or as spectators. In many instances a coach will transport a group of boys in his own car to observe athletic events at another school or to a college event.

One factor which will affect the decision of the court involves the statutes regarding injuries incurred while riding in the car of another. This will vary from state to state and it would be wise for anyone planning to perform such a function to review this area. In an Idaho case in which a coach directed a group of boys to ride with him to a contest in a car which he had borrowed from another teacher, during the trip the coach had an accident and the car rolled down an embankment, resulting in an injury to one of the boys riding with him. The parents of the boy brought suit against the owner of the car contending the coach had been negligent and the owner of the car was therefore liable. In Idaho there does exist a "guest statute" whereby anyone who rides in a car in a "guest" status cannot sue the owner of the vehicle. In this instance, however, the coach had directed the student to ride in the car to the athletic contest and he was thus not a "guest" in the true sense of the word.[19]

There was another recent litigation in Delaware which would definitely set a precedent in legal decisions regarding the transportation of students in privately owned vehicles. A child was injured in a school playground during the noon hour and a teacher drove the youngster home.

[19] *Gorton vs. Doty*, 57 Idaho, 792, 69 P. 2d 136 (1937).

The child was absent from school and the teacher became concerned over the seriousness of the injury. On going to the youngster's home the teacher discovered there had been no means of transportation for the youngster to get to the doctor. The teacher volunteered to drive the student and his mother to the doctor and during the trip they were involved in an accident in which both the mother and the child were injured. Both of the injured parties sued the teacher for damages. The counsel for the defense contended the teacher was performing an errand of mercy and the two passengers were "guests" in the teacher's car as it was not her obligation to perform this service. The court, however, indicated it felt the teacher had a moral obligation and due to this act of kindness she would be improving herself as a teacher. As a "guest" of the teacher in her car the injured parties could not have sued the driver, according to the state's "guest statute" but since the court did not consider these individuals as "guests" they were allowed to make such claims against the teacher. This may appear as a rather broad interpretation as to what will benefit a teacher in his or her professional development but it does stand on the court record as such.[20]

The use of a privately owned vehicle resulted in an unusual situation in Kansas. A girl was injured in an automobile accident while riding to an athletic contest at another school during school hours. The driver of the car, another student, had the permission of his father to use his car for such a trip. The school became involved only because it had permitted the girl to ride to the game. Although the school had not paid for the car's use, the vehicle was still under its control and on this basis the legal action had been instituted against the driver and not the owner of the car. School permission precluded the "guest" statute in this state.[21]

---

[20] *Truitt vs. Gaines,* 318 F. (2d) 461 (Delaware, 1963).
[21] *Kitzel vs. Atkenson,* 245 P. (2d) 170 (Kansas, 1952).

In a very similar situation a cheerleader was being transported to an athletic contest in a private car. The athletic director knew of such an arrangement and thus implied school approval. However, the court felt that such passengers were "guests" and the school was not involved.[22]

Coaches or directors of athletic programs must realize the courts have some unusual views on this matter of transportation injuries. Most individuals in such positions can probably recall incidents in which they have exposed themselves to possible expensive legal action if even a minor accident had occurred.

There are numerous factors which must be considered in transportation including the legality of using public funds, safety of the vehicles, competence of the drivers, immunity from tort liability for transportation accidents, overloading of vehicles, the use of privately owned vehicles and the "guest statutes" which are applicable in the various states.

---

[22] *Fessenden vs. Smith,* 124 N.W. (2d) 554 (Iowa, 1964).

8

The Legal Aspects of Insurance

IN DISCUSSING THE LEGAL ASPECTS OF INSURANCE AS RELATED
to athletics there are two basic types which must be considered: liability and accident. Both have a relationship to
athletics but there are distinct variations in regulations
from state to state due to the existing statutes.

Liability

The basic purpose behind liability insurance as carried
by school districts is to protect them from a loss of public
funds through legal action. Although school districts are
immune from lawsuits in many states, a number of such
units do carry liability insurance. At one extreme the purchase of such protection is held illegal, while at the other
it is required by law. Some states hold it as a legal expenditure under specific statutes or through a broad interpretation of the law. The purchase of liability insurance may
appear to be inconsistent with the implications of immunity, but due to recent court judgments school district
officers realize that such immunity may not long be considered as being applicable in all situations. In order to protect public funds, therefore, it would appear as though
the officers of such groups have considered it prudent to
carry such protection in the event of their immunity's suddenly being removed.

111

In reference to specific variations, California, for example, seems to be the only state at this time which actually requires that school districts carry liability insurance to cover all school activities. In fourteen states (Connecticut, Illinois, Massachusetts, Minnesota, New Hampshire, New Jersey, New Mexico, New York, North Carolina, Oregon, Pennsylvania, South Dakota, Washington and Wyoming) permissive legislation allows school districts to pay the premiums for liability insurance from public funds. In the states of Arkansas, Idaho, Iowa, North Dakota and Vermont statutes allow governmental units to purchase liability insurance from public funds, and under a broad interpretation of these regulations school districts are permitted to purchase such insurance. In several states the courts have indicated that since a school is permitted to carry liability insurance the injured party has the right to make a claim on a school district, as the protective policy was purchased by public money. In the states of Minnesota, Oregon, Tennessee, Kentucky and Illinois the plaintiff has been allowed to make a claim on the school districts to the extent of the liability coverage. This is a reasonable approach to the problem and might well prove to be the trend in the near future. Such an interpretation, however, does not necessarily waive immunity for the school district, but will provide a method of recourse for the injured party in those school districts which utilize public money for such protection.

In the states of Kansas, Ohio and Georgia the only liability insurance coverage allowable is that which covers transportation. This may indicate another trend whereby states recognize that certain activities tend to create more hazardous situations than do others and might well consider it reasonable to allow school districts to purchase liability insurance and permit claims for negligent actions in such activities. These might include transportation, athletics, physical education, manual training and the like.

Delaware, Mississippi, Texas and West Virginia will not permit school districts to purchase any liability protection as the statutes specifically indicate that such an expenditure of public funds is illegal.

There have been a few litigations in this area of insurance and these tend to support the interpretations of the state laws. Even though a school district does carry liability insurance this does not necessarily remove their immunity from legal action. In one particular case in New Mexico the courts indicated that a public institution could not be sued for negligence due to its immunity, even though the plaintiff merely wished to establish the amount of damages that might be collected from the insurance company which carried the institution's liability insurance.[1]

There was a similar case in Pennsylvania in which the plaintiff attempted to sue a school district since it carried liability insurance. Once again the courts found that a school district was immune from such a suit even though it carried liability insurance.[2]

There was a legal action in West Virginia concerning the purchase of liability insurance by a board of education. There was a change in the membership of this board and the new group attempted to obtain a rebate on liability insurance premiums purchased by the preceding board. The courts found in favor of the board of education, indicating that unless authorized by statute, such a group could not purchase liability insurance to protect itself against non-existing liability.[3]

There are states in which the courts have indicated the purpose behind the immunity from legal action is to protect public money. If a school district does carry liability

---

[1] *Livingston vs. New Mexico College of A & M Arts,* 328 P. (2d) 79 (New Mexico, 1958).

[2] *Supler vs. School District of North Franklin Township,* 182 A (2d) 535 (Pennsylvania, 1962).

[3] *Board of Education of the County of Raleigh vs. Commercial Casualty Insurance Co.,* 116 W. Va. 503, 182 S.E. 87 (1935).

insurance then this danger is removed and the school district can thus be named in such a suit as long as the claim does not exceed the coverage. This decision was reached in the courts of both Oregon and Illinois.[4,5]

Liability for transportation accidents has been approached with viewpoints which may differ radically from those involving other school activities. This is obvious from the variations in state laws when compared to the statutes applicable to other facets of the school program. Twenty-two states require that school districts carry liability insurance on transportation, eighteen specifically indicate that it is allowable expenditure, four make it permissive and in two states it is not clearly defined. There are only four states which specifically indicate it is an illegal expenditure. It was indicated earlier that certain states do make allowances for transportation accidents and make it possible for claims to be made against specific funds set aside for this purpose. Obviously state governments have considered that transportation is more likely to result in student injuries than other activities and have made concessions to protect school districts and their pupils in this area.

School districts in many states may purchase spectator liability insurance to cover athletic events. In some states this would not be necessary due to school immunity, while in other instances the regular liability insurance carried by the school district would provide the necessary coverage. If a school district leases a facility for an athletic contest it would be advisable to verify whether the fee charged includes spectator liability insurance or if this must be purchased separately. This precaution is most prevalent during tournament play when larger community or college owned facilities are utilized.

---

[4] *Vendrell vs. School District No. 26 Malheur County,* 360 P. (2d) 282 (Oregon, 1961).
[5] *Thomas vs. Broadlands Community Consolidated School District,* 348 Illinois App. 567, 109 N.E. 2d 636 (1952).

In an earlier chapter the importance of individual liability insurance was mentioned. In all states it is legal for coaches to purchase such insurance. Due to the increase in legal actions involving individuals associated with athletics, a number of insurance companies have made individual liability coverage available to such groups. It would be advisable to verify the legality and the coverage of such policies. In those states which are immune from litigation and have no "save harmless" provisions to protect the individual teacher, the purchase of such a policy might be a wise move. Many professional groups such as the American Association of Health, Physical Education and Recreation, and a number of state teachers' associations provide their members with the opportunity of purchasing such protection at a low group rate. Several state education associations provide such protection as one of the benefits of membership. Leibee indicates such insurance protection ranges from $10,000 to $100,000.[6]

Accident Insurance

The attitude toward accident insurance varies considerably from state to state. Many allow the purchase of athletic insurance to protect those students participating in athletics from medical costs. In some states the premiums may be paid from public money, while in others the cost of such premiums must come from athletic funds. Louisiana, for example, allows accident insurance for those participating in athletics, but it is specifically stated that the cost of the premiums may come only from athletic funds. In a few states it is legal to provide accident insurance for all pupils in all school activities with the cost of such coverage legally expended from public funds. In many it is legal for the school districts to provide an opportunity for students, including athletes, to purchase their own accident insurance.

The National Federation of State High School Athletic

---

[6] Leibee, Howard. *Tort Liability for Injuries to Pupils*, p. 31

Associations Handbook indicates there are a number of ways in which the states provide the opportunity for athletes to obtain athletic insurance. In some this accident benefit plan is a part of the high school athletic association's program, while in others the state associations have incorporated athletic benefit companies to administer the athletic insurance program. Other state associations will designate a particular insurance company to administer the program for all high schools in the state and thus provide them with financial savings. In some instances several companies may be designated as the approved agents for such a program, while in others there may be no such designation and the schools are free to vie for themselves.

In a recent interpretation by the legal counsel of the Education Department in New York State it was indicated the sale of a specific accident insurance plan throughout the school was illegal in this state. After several discussions on this question it would appear as though the school or its employees would be considered as acting as agents for the particular company. The counsel indicated it was illegal to use a captive audience in an attempt to sell a school-wide plan. Oddly enough it would be legal for the school district to purchase with public funds such a plan to cover all the students.

It is becoming more common for school districts to require that all athletes be covered by accident insurance. It is questionable if a boy could be restricted from participation if this matter were brought before the court. If the athlete was not covered by such insurance and he wished to participate, and met all other eligibility requirements, any injury due to the inherent danger of the activity could be considered as the responsibility of the participant. This precludes, of course, any negligence. An interpretation of the Education Law in New York clearly stated that a boy could not be denied the right to participate in athletics or other such activities because he had not purchased accident insurance.

9

The Legality of Eligibility Standards Determined by Local School Officials

MANY SCHOOLS IMPOSE SPECIFIC ELIGIBILITY STANDARDS TO which the student athletes must adhere. There are frequent controversial discussions as to whether participation in athletics is a right or a privilege for the students. These discussions may be merely a matter of interpretation of semantics rather than a true disagreement on viewpoints. Participation in athletics is a right for those students who have adhered to the eligibility requirements determined by the school administration or employees who are responsible for the activity. In this vein it might be said it is a privilege which must be earned through proper conduct. No matter what the viewpoint, the important factor here is the legality of school personnel in determining such standards. These standards are usually based upon scholastic achievement, conduct and other pertinent areas.

Referring once again to the legal viewpoint expounded by Dr. John Jehu, Director of the Division of Law, New York State Education Department: he was asked the question, "Is it legal for a school district board of education to install a system of eligibility for extra-class activity based upon scholastic activity only?"

Dr. Jehu's reply:

This is a difficult question to answer because a board

117

of education through its personnel including you people [athletic directors], of course, has certain powers of discipline. Discipline is a difficult thing to use because different pupils respond differently (and in some cases not at all) to different types of attempts to bring to bear some discipline. I don't believe you can exclude a young-ster from required physical education anymore than you can say, as a matter of discipline or because your marks are falling off, we are not going to teach you math anymore. That you may not do. On the other hand there are certain extra curricular activities, shall we say, that the youngsters are very fond of participating in. They are not required. As to those I think a reasonable amount of exclusion can be exercised by the board of education, superintendent, principal or whoever it is in order to induce the youngster to do what he ought to be doing. Now there are a lot of pupils who do not care about any of the various subjects but you exclude them from the extra class activities and you hit them where it hurts and consequently this is one way of handling some of these situations. But I don't think you exclude them from those which are required as a matter of law.[1]

It would appear, according to Dr. Jehu's interpretation, that a local eligibility system is perfectly legal.

The Wisconsin Interscholastic Athletic Association deemed it advisable to obtain the opinion of the Attorney General of the state in such matters and he has indicated the following interpretations:

1. School authorities have power to impose reasonable regulations which must be observed by the pupils as a prerequisite to engaging in interscholastic competition. If the school board does not adopt rules and regulations which cover the subject matter, the principal or super-vising teacher may do so.

[1] Report of the Statewide Conference for School District Directors of Health, Physical Education and Recreation, State Education Department Building, Nov. 15–16, 1962.

2. Matters which directly affect the safe and orderly operation and functioning of an athletic program may be made the subject of a rule or regulation even though they might relate to matters other than scholastic standing or conduct during school hours.

3. All male pupils desiring to compete for a place on athletic teams sponsored by the school must comply with all reasonable rules and regulations adopted by school authorities relating thereto.

The same individual was asked specific questions regarding this matter of eligibility as follows:

"May such rules prohibit a pupil's eligibility to compete in interscholastic competition for any cause arising outside of scholastic standing and conduct in school hours?"

"Yes. — School authorities are not required to sponsor interscholastic athletic competition and if they do so they have power to impose reasonable rules and regulations which must be observed as a prerequisite to engaging in such competition. Matters which directly affect the safe, orderly and proper operation and functioning of an athletic program may be made the subject of a rule or regulation even though they might relate to matters other than scholastic standing or conduct during school hours."

"Is an amateur pupil of a public school, in good scholastic standing and not guilty of misconduct during the school hours, entitled as a matter of law to compete for a place on a school sponsored team?"

"The constitutional right of every child to attend school is not absolute. It is subject to reasonable regulations by the school authorities or legislature. For purpose of this opinion, it may be assumed that all male pupils have a right to compete on an equal basis for a place on athletic teams sponsored by the school but, as already pointed out in this opinion, the school is not obliged to sponsor inter-scholastic athletic competition and if those in charge decide to do so, they may establish reasonable rules and regulations which must be complied with as a prerequisite to engaging in such competition and may include therein matters which directly affect the safe, orderly and proper operation of an athletic program even though they might relate to matters other than scholastic standing or conduct during school hours, and any boy desiring to compete would be obliged to comply therewith."

The Attorney General supported his interpretations by citing the judgment of the courts when he stated, "Pupils may be forbidden from engaging in designated athletic activities, as playing football, either on or away from school grounds." This judgment was quoted from the case of *Kinzer vs. Torns,* 129 Iowa 441, 105 N.W. 686, 3 L.R.A. 496.

He also cited the case of *O'Rourke vs. Walker,* 102 Conn., 130, 129 Atl. 25, 41 A.L.R., which also supported the contention. Both the previous cases were used as precedent setting decisions in the case of *Dresser vs. the District Board,* which was similar in vein.

The only possible interpretation, since there are several precedent-setting decisions appearing on the court records, would seem to indicate it is perfectly within the rights of the school board, the administration or the individual responsible for an athletic activity to determine specific eligibility standards for those participating in school-sponsored athletic activities.

The Eligibility of Married Students

There were two other legal actions which involved slightly different problems arising from local eligibility rules. Those had to do with the right of a school board to eliminate married students from participating in interscholastic athletics. In the first case a married student sought to compel the school board to allow him to participate in basketball despite a ruling which they had made eliminating all married students from such participation. The counsel for the plaintiff indicated this individual was being discriminated against due to his marital status. The court supported the contention of the school board, indicating there were a number of factors which made it inadvisable for a married student to participate. It felt an athlete is held in some esteem by the student body and his actions are often emulated. His attendance at practice sessions and games would also detract from his ability to support a wife. Finally, approval of participation might indicate that the school board condoned teenage marriages, which, of course, was far from the truth.[2]

The second legal action was similar in nature; a married student was denied the right to participate in wrestling and baseball. The plaintiff contended in this action that this prohibition did not encompass other activities in the school and therefore discriminated against him as an athlete. The court contended the other areas which he mentioned were held during school hours and were connected with credit-gaining courses. They also indicated a school board had the right to determine fair eligibility regulations for athletic participation and this regulation did not appear to them to be discriminatory. As in the previous case the court indicated the school board should not encourage teenage marriages and this was one method of indicating such mar-

---

[2] *Baker vs. Stevenson,* 189 N.E. (2d) 181 (Ohio, 1962).

riages were not met with approval. They also reiterated that once such responsibilities were assumed by the students, in order to fulfill financial obligations which accompany marriage, their time should not be consumed by extracurricular activities.[3]

These two cases further support the contention that the courts feel school boards can set certain eligibility requirements, even in a rather broad area, for participation in interscholastic athletics.

---

[3] *Starkey vs. Board of Education of Davis County School District,* 381 P. (2d) 718 (Utah, 1963).

10

Equal Competition

THE MATTER OF EQUAL COMPETITION MUST BE APPROACHED from two viewpoints: individual and team. The first deals with the matching of individuals in athletic activities. There are certain activities that by their nature will match one individual against another in physical contact. Wrestling, boxing, judo and activities of this type would fall into this category; and the maturity and size of the individuals would certainly have a telling effect upon the decisions of the courts in the event of litigations.

For example, wrestling has specific weight classes which set limitations as to the weight variation between contestants. As the sport grows there are more and more regulations included by the state athletic associations to guarantee equal competition. Weight classifications are an important factor in such a sport, and there are situations in which this weight consideration could have resulted in liability claims. The usual regulations clearly state that an individual must not be over a specific weight to wrestle in a particular class, but in many areas there is still no regulation which forbids a boy from participating in a weight class well above his own weight. If a boy of 130 pounds were injured while wrestling another at 160 pounds there is no doubt the courts would take a rather dim view. Although this practice might not be strictly illegal according to the regulations, it might still be considered a negligent act. To prevent such an occurrence many state athletic associations have included a regulation which forbids a boy from wrestling more than one or two classes above his normal weight. This, however, will vary from state to state.

Another situation which can occur in sports such as wrestling, boxing or judo would be unequal competition at the unlimited class. Although the lower weight classes have definite restrictions, the unlimited class may not. Assuming the second heaviest classification sets a limit at 180 pounds, a boy over this weight must wrestle in the unlimited class. This places no limit on the weight of the competitors over 180 pounds and there have been situations where a boy approximately 190 pounds would be wrestling another of 300 pounds. Once again the rules may permit this but the attitude of the courts may not coincide with such regulations. Since high school athletic associations realize that such inequalities may exist there has been some action to add another weight class, such as the addition of a superheavyweight class for boys who are extremely heavy. Another positive move in this direction has been to limit the difference in weight between two competitors in either the heavyweight or the super-heavyweight classification.

There was a court case which was based upon this matter of equal competition. Two boys were allowed by a physical education teacher to engage in a boxing match, even though neither had any training in the sport of boxing. The event turned into a slugging match with one boy obviously much superior to the other. The overmatched boy was fatally injured. The parents instituted a suit against the instructor and the courts found in favor of the plaintiffs. The following statement is from the court record in this case:

It is the duty of a teacher to exercise reasonable care

to prevent injuries. Pupils should be warned before being permitted to engage in a dangerous and hazardous exercise. These young men should have been taught the principle of defense if indeed it was a reasonable thing to permit a slugging match of the kind which the testimony indicates that the teacher failed in his duties in this regard and that he was negligent, and the plaintiff is entitled to recover.[1]

In another instance a coach who used a more prudent approach matched two boys in a wrestling match. He compared their weights, studied their comparative ability, and supervised the match. One of the youngsters was injured, and in the legal action that followed the courts felt the coach had used discretion and found no negligence.[2]

There are certain situations in a team activity over which the supervisor will have control and it is up to this individual to protect the safety of the participants by guaranteeing competition as reasonable as possible. Assuming a coach is organizing a scrimmage and the activity involved will require physical contact between participants, he must be certain to control this matter of equality in order to protect himself from possible legal action.

A case of note, which has a bearing on any future such legal actions, had to do with the matching of two soccer teams. An extremely large boy collided with one who was much smaller in stature, resulting in a serious injury to the smaller boy. Despite the fact that the boys were in junior high school it was the court's contention the supervisor could have prevented such an injury if he had used discretion in organizing the teams. Thus he was guilty of negligence.[3]

---

[1] *LeValley vs. Stanford,* 272 App. Div. 183, 70 N.Y.S. 2d 460 (1947).
[2] *Reynolds vs. State,* 207 Misc. (N.Y.), 1963, 141 N.Y. Supp. 2d 615 (1955).
[3] *Brooks vs. Board of Education of New York City,* 205 N.Y.S. (2d) 777 (New York, 1960).

On the other hand the courts do recognize that completely equal competition is rather idealistic. If this were the case then all athletic events would end in tied scores. There is no doubt there will be a variation in the abilities of the boys participating and the superior team will usually win the contest. This was the basis of a litigation in Oregon where a fifteen-year-old boy participating in a high school football game was tackled by two larger boys from an opposing team. The boy received a broken neck and was permanently injured. When he reached legal age he sued the school district, indicating the team on which he played had been overmatched and he had not received sufficient coaching. The courts indicated that in athletic contests one team is usually superior to another and this was no basis for litigation. As quoted from the court record:

> Although the complainant alleges that the Vale team contained "large and rough" boys, there is nothing to negate the idea that the Nyssa team also contained "large and rough" boys, albeit inexperienced. It is our opinion that the allegations do not describe a breach of duty on the part of the school district or its agents or servants. The playing of football is a body-contact sport. There is no other way to play it. No prospective player need be told that a participant may sustain injury. The fact is self-evident.[4]

Obviously neither a coach nor the other employees of the school district should cancel an athletic contest simply because the outlook is rather foreboding. If this were the case the entire basis of high school athletics would be disrupted. In most areas leagues and competition are organized on the basis of relatively equal enrollment of students and with the assumption that if one school has some "rough and tough" players, a school of approximately equal size

[4] *Vendrell vs. School District No. 260 Malheur County,* 376 p 2d 406 (Oregon, 1962).

might well have a comparable number of such endowed individuals.

When it comes to equal competition, the coach, in certain instances, can regulate the matching of opponents, but there are situations in which it cannot be considered as negligence since the supervisor has no control over such conditions.

11

Athletic Awards

A STUDY OF THE LAW AND ATHLETICS MUST INCLUDE INFOR-
mation on awards since there have been legal actions concerned with this area. As mentioned earlier, it is illegal in
many states to purchase equipment for athletic teams from
public money and this restriction would also prohibit the
purchase of awards with such money. In those states where
it is legal to purchase athletic equipment with school funds
there is always the question of whether athletic awards can
be included in this broad term of "equipment." It would
seem there might be some question as to the legality of
spending tax money for such items.

In New York a rather unusual situation developed a
few years ago. The Education Law clearly states that no
school money may be spent on awards of any type. However, the method of handling school funds was recently
revised and all money collected from the gate receipts of
athletic events must be deposited in the general school
fund. By adhering to the law this would immediately
eliminate the possibility of purchasing athletic awards.
After several interpretations it was concluded such items
could be purchased with school funds if they were included
as a budget item. In those states where gate receipts are
placed in a separate athletic fund, there would be little
question as to the legality of such an expenditure.

Limitations on Awards

According to the *National Federation of State High School Athletic Associations Handbook,* there is considerable variation in award limitations. Excluding such awards as medals, only letters may be awarded in Delaware, Idaho, Iowa, Kansas, Nebraska, Nevada, Ohio, Oregon, Washington and Wisconsin. Obviously no other awards are legal in these states. There is a definite limit to the value of the awards which may be presented, varying from one dollar to five dollars, in the states of Alabama, Arizona, Colorado, Delaware, Florida, Idaho, Illinois, Kentucky, Maryland, Michigan, Minnesota, Missouri, Montana, Nevada, New Mexico, North Dakota, Ohio, Pennsylvania, South Dakota, Tennessee, Utah, Virginia, West Virginia, Wisconsin and Wyoming.

Those states not listed either set no limit, ignore any restrictions or have completely different limitations. The National Federation recommends that an athlete should not accept an award of any nature which exceeds a value of one dollar except for those usually presented—such as medals, trophies, fobs, letters and other athletic insignia. Such a statement is still rather broad in nature, as it seems to set no limit on the usual type of award.

This question was raised in Wisconsin and the Attorney General supplied this interpretation:

> "May a pupil be declared a professional athlete for receiving an award less than $35 in value?"
> "Yes, a rule which prohibits a professional athlete from competing in interscholastic high school athletic competition is reasonable. In enforcing such a rule, it is necessary to set up standards to determine when a pupil is or is not a professional athlete. In doing this, it would be perfectly proper to declare that any pupil who receives any award of more than nominal value shall be

considered a professional as otherwise a most obvious loophole would exist, in that an athlete could be paid by the simple expedient of giving him awards of a value which then can be turned into money."

There seems to be only one case brought before the courts which dealt directly with eligibility and awards. Actually the basic premise behind this case was a test as to whether a state athletic association could declare an individual ineligible for participation due to the acceptance of an award which was beyond the limitations set by this association. The members of a rather successful football team in Oklahoma were presented with small gold footballs. Those who had received these awards were declared ineligible by the Oklahoma High School Athletic Association as this was in direct opposition to this association's regulations. One of the individuals involved attempted to have the courts revoke this penalty, with the main contention being that such an association did not have the right to inflict such a penalty. The case went as far as the Oklahoma Supreme Court, which decided that the state association had a right to penalize the individual for disregarding the regulation. Oddly enough the court reached this decision even though those involved had returned the awards well in advance of the court case.[1]

In the next chapter much of the information will deal with the legality of state athletic associations' doling out penalties for a violation of their regulations. This particular case indicates the courts are willing to accept the judgment of such associations in determining the types and cost of such awards.

A rather unusual and what may seem an unfair judgment on awards by a state association occurred in Texas in 1964. A high school football team had an outstanding sea-

---

[1] *Morrison vs. Roberts*, 183 Okla. 359, 82 Pac. 2d 1023 (Oklahoma, 1938).

son and was honored by the community. The members were awarded lettered jackets by the school. In addition a church in the community presented each boy with a copy of *Play Ball,* published by the Fellowship of Christian Athletes, which is a book of religious testimonials by nationally famous athletes. The Texas Interscholastic League sets a limit on awards of $15 and the price of the jackets equalled this amount. By accepting the $2.95 book, which had a religious theme, the members of the team had broken an association rule. Even though they returned the books when the matter was brought to light, the school was placed on probation for three years.[2]

---

[2] "Scorecard," *Sports Illustrated*, Volume 23, No. 2, July 12, 1965.

12

The Legal Aspects of State Athletic Associations

THERE HAVE BEEN SEVERAL LEGAL ACTIONS WHICH HAVE involved state athletic associations and most of these were concerned with the right of such organizations to control high school athletics. Before entering into a discussion of these legal actions, however, it might be wise to take a brief look into the history of the various types of state athletic associations.

These associations take one of three forms. The first group comprises the voluntary organizations and proves to be the most prevalent type. Here, the schools control the organization, as they elect representatives and determine the rules and regulations of the group. They are free to revise the regulations as they see fit and as circumstances change.

The second group is made up of those associations which are affiliated with state education departments. This arrangement considerably strengthens the state association's powers, as the regulations of the education department are part of the law and the schools in the state are bound to adhere to such regulations.

The third type of organization is the university-directed association. These groups are under the direction of large universities in their particular states and it can be presumed the original assumption was that a university group would have more experience in this field of athletic control and could better administer such a program.

The organization of state athletic associations had its beginning as early as 1895, when interested school groups created such associations in Wisconsin and Illinois. Since that time all fifty states have formulated similar associations. The basic purpose behind such groups was to develop controls over the eligibility regulations for the various athletic activities. Without such a controlling body there would be a hodgepodge of divergent regulations which could only result in mass confusion as various high school athletic teams attempted to schedule events. With no such athletic control high school groups could well decide upon their own set of regulations, which would result in hundreds of variations, formulated with only local circumstances in mind.

There is no doubt the organizers of the state associations realized that a lack of control in high school athletics would eventually lead to their complete downfall. Such foresighted individuals had complete faith in the values of high school athletics, and in order to guarantee the future success of athletics at this level organized a common set of eligibility requirements to which the schools would have to adhere if they wished to participate with state association schools. At the outset chaotic conditions still existed and the eligibility regulations were frequently ignored, but these groups continued to grow in strength down through the years and at the present time exert almost complete control over high school athletic eligibility regulations in the various states. These associations are most concerned with standardized rules of play, restrictions on sport seasons, minimum eligibility standards, the guarantee of equal competition, and settling disputes between member schools.

As the state groups began to exert more control over their high school athletic programs, certain individuals visualized a national group which would further strengthen the state associations. In 1920 a group of Midwestern state associations took the first steps in the organization of the National Federation of State High School Athletic Associations. The purpose of the group was not to exert control over the state associations but rather to aid them in improving their own local situations and provide some regulations for interstate competition. This group could also act as the spokesman for the state associations in problems which were national in scope, such as relationships with the colleges and universities, and with professional baseball, football and basketball groups. Even today, although its strength has grown considerably, the National Federation still only "recommends" and does not try to force its opinion upon the member states. The National Federation's recommendations are the result of the information garnered from the various state associations who have solved problems which may be plaguing other associations. At the present time 49 of the 50 states are members of the National Federation, and four neighboring Canadian provinces are affiliated members.

Mutual Legal Aid Pact

One of the most important functions of the National Federation is the maintenance of a mutual legal aid pact. Through this arrangement any association which experiences legal difficulties may obtain, from the National Federation, a large number of briefs concerning legal actions which have involved other state associations. In such actions these will supply the involved association with court decisions which could be precedent-setting in nature and support the contentions of such an association in exerting its controls over high school athletics.

In the *National Federation Handbook,* this problem of legal action against state associations is somewhat clarified in the following quote:

Court action against a state association has been initiated by plaintiffs who have objected to enforcement of some eligibility or contest rule. Several lower courts have ruled in favor of the plaintiff. Temporary injunctions or adverse lower court rulings have occurred in twelve states. In each case, the injunction has been dissolved after a hearing or the adverse decision has been reversed by a higher court. In Colorado, Indiana, Florida, North Dakota, Ohio, Oklahoma, Texas and West Virginia, cases have been carried to the State Supreme Court. Each has resulted in a decision that a State High School Association, in common with any other reputable voluntary organization, has the right to enforce any reasonable regulation to which its members have subscribed as one of the conditions of membership.[1]

The Right to Impose Penalties

In 1949 the Attorney General of Wisconsin clearly indicated his opinions regarding the controls which could be exerted by state athletic associations:

Where school authorities by proper action take necessary steps which result in the school becoming members of a voluntary association which has established certain basic rules or regulations regarding the conduct of interscholastic athletic competition, the effect is to make the rules or regulations of that association those of the school. So far as the individual pupil is concerned such rules and regulations are those of the school and he must comply with them to compete. The school authorities have power to judge and determine facts as to whether the pupil has failed to comply with a rule or regulation and to discipline him accordingly, without permitting the pupil a hearing.

---

[1] *National Federation of State High School Athletic Associations Handbook,* 1964–65 Edition, p. 41.

There is no legal objection to the imposition of a so-called "Fine" under a provision of the constitution of a voluntary association to the effect that a member school shall be subject to the imposition of a fine if, through a violation of the rules of the association or otherwise, the association is caused extra expense, in an amount sufficient to reimburse it for such expense, it being assumed that the money used to pay the so-called "fine" will come from the receipts of the interscholastic athletic events. (This of course will vary from state to state dependent upon the Education Law— Author.)

Denial or revocation of other privileges of membership of a voluntary association on ground of violation of the rules imposed in accordance with the constitution or by-laws of the association would be proper if the particular penalty was applied under the circumstances of each is reasonable.

This interpretation, along with several precedent-setting court decisions, seems to indicate that joining such an organization is purely voluntary and the sole objective of such groups is the improvement of high school athletics through standardization of regulations. A school which joins such an organization should fully understand the regulations and rules of the group and realize that membership implies they will adhere to these regulations and rules. If they do not do so then it is within the legal rights of the state associations to penalize the offending school.

There have been several instances where this premise has been questioned and, as mentioned, there were decisions in favor of the plaintiffs in cases against state associations in lower courts. Fortunately for high school athletics, higher courts have reversed such decisions and supported the right of state associations to enforce their penalties.

Legal Actions Involving Athletic Associations

A most involved case occurred in Ohio where the final step was an attempt by the Attorney General to abolish the Ohio High School Athletic Association. The problem began when a large high school in the state seemingly "imported" two football players, who were brothers, from another school. The two boys had reported for practice at the original school when their father suddenly "found" a better position in the neighboring community. It would appear, however, his employer was the President of the "Boosters Club" in the new school. The school from which the boys came sent a protest to the O.H.S.A.A., and as a result of investigation the state association suspended the supposedly "recruiting" school for one year. An injunction was obtained to eliminate the enforcement of this suspension, thereby making it mandatory that schools belonging to the state association complete their contractual agreements. The legal counsel for the state association countered by attempting to have a higher court refute the injunction, but was unable to do so. The next action was taken by the Attorney General's office, which attempted to have the O.H.S.A.A. abolished, indicating the controls which this organization held over the various high schools was truly a function of the local boards of education. It was implied that this group was infringing upon the powers of the boards of education and they had no legal right to demand that the individual schools adhere to their regulations. Fortunately, the higher courts, in the ensuing legal action, found in favor of the O.H.S.A.A. and further strengthened the power of this and other state athletic associations to exert control over high school athletics.[2]

Another rather involved case concerned a high school in

---

[2] *Physical Education Newsletter,* Letter 10, Vol. 6, January 27, 1962, Croft Educational Services, New London, Conn.

Florida. Two high schools had been competing against each other for several years. Even though there was a type of contractual agreement, one school severed relations with the other and refused to play the football game which was scheduled for that fall. The offended school turned to the state association's Executive Secretary, who ruled there was no actual contractual agreement and it was not necessary for the schools to meet. Although the offended school had the right to appeal this decision to the Executive Committee of the association, they chose to take the case to court. The court was in agreement with the Executive Secretary's decision and indicated the game need not be played. Since the school had not utilized the association's procedure for appeal but had taken the case to court, the school was suspended for violation of the regulations. Once again the school instituted legal action in an attempt to set aside the suspension by the state association. A temporary injunction allowed the school to participate in two games but the court then decided the suspension had been in order. The school took the case to the Florida Supreme Court which upheld the suspension, indicating this action was an internal affair of the association.[3]

In 1953 there was a litigation in Texas over the right of an interscholastic association to enforce one of its regulations which would have resulted in the cancellation of a high school all-star game. In this particular situation Midwestern University had leased the stadium belonging to the Wichita Falls School District for its home games. The University had been doing so for several years, and in addition to its home games had sponsored a high school all-star football game involving players from both Texas and Oklahoma. The University Interscholastic League, of which Wichita Falls was a member, adopted a regulation which prohibited the use of school facilities or school per-

---

[3] *Sult vs. Gilbert,* 3 Southern 2d 729 (Florida, 1941).

sonnel for such all star games. Wichita Falls indicated to Midwestern University it would be illegal for it to permit the all-star game to be played on its field due to this new regulation. Midwestern contended it had contracted for the use of the field, that the all-star game should be considered as one of its season games, and should not concern the school district since it was not the sponsoring group. After a meeting with both the school and league officials these groups indicated they would not permit this all-star game to take place in the high school stadium. The University took legal action and a lower court issued an injunction which would permit the game to be played. The school district and the league appealed the case but the injunction was upheld in the court of appeals. The case then moved to the State Supreme Court where it was adjudged there was no question as to the legality of the contract for Midwestern University to use the stadium for its regular-season games; but in the court's judgment the all-star game could not be considered a regular-season game. As a voluntary member of the University Interscholastic League, Wichita Falls was required to adhere to the regulations of this group and could not allow its stadium to be used for an all-star game of this nature.[4]

Once again the highest court of a state reversed a decision of the lower courts. This was also a reiteration of the fact that a school district which joins a voluntary organization is cognizant of its regulations before doing so, and in agreeing to join such a group indicates it will adhere to such regulations.

Although the following case is not directly related to athletics it does indicate that voluntary associations have the right to terminate the membership of any member who does not meet the qualifications of the group. A state agricultural college in North Dakota was removed from mem-

---

[4] *University Interscholastic League vs. Midwestern University,* 250 Southwestern 587 (Texas, 1953).

bership in an association of colleges and secondary schools. The purpose of this group was to certify that member schools measured up to certain standards and could be considered as satisfactory educational institutions. This particular institution was judged not to have maintained the standards as required by the association and were dropped from membership. The case was decided by a court of appeals and it indicated that a voluntary organization of this type could determine the qualifications of its members and could expel such members for not maintaining the standards required.[5]

The case of *Morrison vs. Roberts* in Oklahoma which involved the acceptance of an award in excess of those stipulated by the state athletic association was mentioned in the previous chapter. In this case the plaintiff attempted to have his eligibility reinstated, contending the penalty had been unduly severe and the award he received had been returned. A district court indicated that the Oklahoma High School Athletic Association should lift the suspension. The association appealed to the State Supreme Court and this court reversed the decision of the lower court. In the opinion of the Supreme Court, the joining of the association by the particular school implied it intended to adhere to the rules of such an association. The penalty of suspension for such an indiscretion was clearly stated and, although it might be considered an arbitrary penalty, there are many such arbitrary decisions and regulations that must be determined by such a group involved in athletics. In addition the higher court indicated that all rules of the organization are under the control of the individual schools and if the majority of such schools felt a particular penalty was unfair it could easily be deleted or changed through a vote of the member schools.[6]

---

[5] *State of North Dakota vs. North Central Association of Colleges and Secondary Schools,* CCA 7, 99 Fec. 2nd, 697 (North Dakota, 1938).
[6] *Morrison vs. Roberts, op. cit.*

A question of eligibility was raised in another Ohio case in which a ninth grade student was allowed to participate for a high school which he did not attend. The boy in question attended a junior high school which included grades up to the ninth. He was listed as being eligible to participate for a high school in the same city which included grades ten through twelve. The complaint was that this boy was not eligible to participate for a school which he did not attend and the state association agreed with this contention. This group declared the boy ineligible and ordered that all winning games in which he had participated be declared forfeits. The case went as far as the court of appeals, and in its judgment the association was within its rights to make such a decision.[7]

There was an unusual case in West Virginia which involved the selection of participants for a championship football game. There were three unbeaten teams in a particular school classification and a board appointed by the state association had to select two of these teams to participate in the championship game. They did so, but a member of the team not selected filed a suit against the association in an attempt to force its participation in the playoff. A trial judge issued an injunction which prohibited the association from declaring the school ineligible to participate. The appeal became quite entangled in the legal interpretations as in West Virginia it was not legal to name the association in such a suit; instead certain officers had to be named in the litigation. It became further confused as most of the individuals involved were not within the jurisdiction of the court in which the suit was instituted. On taking the case to the State Supreme Court this group set aside the injunction and the game was played between the two teams originally designated. After much of the legal confusion was removed the state

---

[7] *Miller vs. Waldorf,* Court of Appeals, Third Appellate Judicial District of Ohio, Hancock County, June 19, 1952.

association did gain certain advantages although the actual question of its right to regulate the high school athletic program in the state was not considered in the final interpretation. As an unincorporated group it was not open to suit in its name, but could only be named through its officers. The court also verified that a lower court could not issue an injunction concerned with activities or individuals not within its jurisdiction.[8]

In the late 1950's there was a case in Indiana very similar to that which had occurred in Ohio regarding eligibility. A particular school "imported" two basketball players from another school. The schools in its league appealed to the state association, which made a thorough study of the situation and declared the boys ineligible. This resulted in a suit before a circuit court, which found in favor of the players and stated that they should be declared eligible. The state association appealed to the State Supreme Court where the lower court's decision was reversed.

As mentioned earlier, there are certain state athletic associations which are in part under the control of the State Education Department. In New York this happens to be the situation and within the past few years a rather unusual situation has developed. It would appear that certain phases of the Education Law relating to interscholastic athletics were contradictory in nature and this was brought forth in certain legal actions against the New York State Public High School Athletic Association. This discrepancy had to do with the restriction on the number of semesters in which a boy could participate in high school athletics. One section of the law indicated a boy might compete for eight consecutive semesters once he became eligible. The state athletic association required that member schools adhere strictly to this regulation. Another section of the Education Law, however, was somewhat contradictory,

---

[8] *West Virginia Secondary School Activities Commission vs. Wagner,* 102 S.E., 2nd 901 (West Virginia, 1958).

indicating a boy was eligible during his four years in high school. Following the first suit, in which a boy was declared eligible by the court, there were several others similar in nature. There were claims that these boys were not allowed to participate even though they had missed one or more semesters due to illness, moving from state to state where regulations varied, and other such reasons. The Board of Regents, which has almost complete control over all phases of the educational system, in an attempt to eliminate the discrepancy in the regulations deleted the word "consecutive," which will now allow a boy to participate in any eight semesters while he is in high school. There is no doubt the intent of this action was in good faith but the situation has resulted in certain devious practices to guarantee that a boy will be able to participate in a semester which extends beyond his eighth.

13

Miscellaneous Legal Problems
in Athletics

THIS SECTION INCLUDES A NUMBER OF LEGAL CASES AND THE interpretations of such cases which might be classified as being miscellaneous in nature. It is extremely broad in scope as such information does not necessarily fit into areas which were presented earlier.

Broadcasting Athletic Contests

The area of broadcasting athletic events has created some legal problems which have, in a few cases, reached the courts. In the first case the legal action was brought by one broadcasting company against another such company in a battle over the right to broadcast high school athletic events. The plaintiff contended since the school district was publicly supported the school board should not be allowed to sell the rights for such broadcasts to one company but that the rights should be considered as in the public domain. The court found in favor of the defendant, indicating such broadcasting was a commodity to sell and the board of education was well within its rights to sell this as it did other items.[1]

[1] *Southwestern Broadcasting Company vs. Oil Center Broadcasting Company,* 210 S.W. 2nd (Texas, 1947).

In the second legal action a broadcasting company named the Colorado High School Activities Association as the defendant in a suit concerning a charge for the right to broadcast high school athletic contests. Under a specific agreement the high schools and the state association shared such profits. The company contended the school district was publicly supported and it had no right to make such a charge. The court, as in the previous case, found that this charge was legal despite the fact that the school was supported by public funds.[2]

In a 1964 ruling in New York the counsel for the New York State Education Department indicated it was illegal for radio stations to include advertising during the broadcast of high school athletic contests, as this was in opposition to the State Constitution. His interpretation concerned the restriction on local governments, which was judged to include school districts, from using either money, property or such for private gain. The inference was that high school athletes, who were using public school facilities and equipment, were being used by radio stations to gain income from the commercials which were included in the broadcasts. It was obvious this would practically eliminate the broadcasting of high school contests in the state as under this ruling the time utilized for this broadcasting would be a complete financial loss to the radio station, unless the schools involved wished to make payment for this time. Although the ruling could be enforced due to this interpretation it was indicated the individual school districts would have to determine the advisability of allowing the situation to continue. Doubtless, few schools eliminated the radio coverage of their games.

---

[2] *Colorado High School Activities Association vs. Uncompangre Broadcasting Co.,* 134 Colorado 131, 300 P. 2d 968 (1956).

Teacher Supervision and Assignments

Many schools consider teacher supervision at athletic contests as an obligation to be shared by members of the faculty. Although it may not be written in the individual contracts it is often considered an unwritten obligation, as the teachers' presence is considered essential for supervising and maintaining order at such activities. There was a test case in California in which a teacher contended he had been hired to teach a particular subject and not to act as a supervisor at extracurricular activities. This case was brought before the court, which indicated teachers were expected to perform further responsibilities than just teaching, and it was within the legal right of the school administration to assign teachers for supervisor duties at extracurricular activities such as athletic events.[3]

In New York assignment to extracurricular activities is clearly defined in an interpretation of the Education Law:

"May a teacher be required to supervise certain extracurricular activities after regular school hours, without additional salary?"

"Yes—an opinion on a New York City case (Halloran Decision #5563—Commissioner of Education), it was stated that a Board of Education may fix the working hours of teachers, subject only to the requirement that they be reasonable and that a Board may assign any work to a teacher within the scope of the teacher's duties whether it is to be performed during or after the regular school hours. Required duties may not include nonteaching services such as janitorial, police or bus driver.

Most boards, however, do pay extra salary for additional extracurricular supervision, such as assisting in coaching sports, etc."[4]

---

[3] *McGrath vs. Burkhard* (California, 1955).

[4] *Handbook of New York State Education Law,* William J. Hageny, N.Y. State School Boards Association, Inc., 1964 revision, Albany, New York, p. 50.

In another legal action concerning the assignment of a teacher to an extracurricular activity, a history teacher at the start of the school year was notified that he would be assigned to supervise a bowling club. This group was not organized on either an interschool or an intramural basis, but was more in the nature of a club activity. The teacher was not expected to coach or teach bowling but was merely expected to maintain discipline. The teacher felt this type of activity was an imposition and indicated he would not accept this assignment. Due to his persistence in this matter the teacher was dismissed. He appealed to the state superintendent who indicated the teacher should be reinstated. His contention was that such assignments were not made reasonably nor equitably among the faculty members, but he did hold that such an assignment was valid. The court, however, indicated the school board had no right, under the powers invested in it, to make such an assignment. Under the regulations it would be legal for a board to assign a teacher coaching or other extracurricular duties which were related to the school program. The court did not consider that a bowling club, organized as it was, was related to the school program as such.[5]

Libel and Slander

Although this situation does not arise very frequently there are cases on record which have to do with the coaching profession. Conditions do arise whereby a coach may make certain statements regarding the personal qualities of other individuals which could result in slander or libel charges. After a particularly important contest a coach may be emotionally upset due to an extremely disappointing loss and make statements that could very easily be interpreted as being derogatory in nature. Such statements may

---

[5] *Pease vs. Millcreek Township School District,* 195A, (2d) 104 (Pennsylvania, 1963).

be directed at coaches, players or officials. Due to the heat of the moment a coach might permit a newspaper reporter to quote him. If these statements appear in print and it can be verified they were made by a particular individual, that individual could very well find himself faced with a legal suit. For his own protection an individual in such a position must be extremely wary of statements which may be quoted. Emotions will often cause individuals to make rash statements which they regret at a later time, and the coaching profession is fraught with such situations.

Conversely, there are times when articles have appeared in publications which slandered both coaches and players and resulted in extensive lawsuits. The most familiar would be the suits involving two prominent college football coaches who sued a leading publishing company for statements which were made in two articles. These resulted in extended litigations and enormous financial settlements.

A basketball coach on the West Coast was awarded $175,000 in 1965 in a libel suit against the same publishing company. An article, which had been written by a former basketball referee, indicated the coach had incited crowds by disagreeing violently with the officials' decisions. The coach's contract was allowed to lapse shortly after the article. He indicated the charges in the article were false and that the notoriety had ruined his career as a basketball coach.

There is one court action on record involving a player who sued a publishing company for implying, in a rather sensational article, that this player was the member of a team which used drugs to increase its performance on the football field. It was proven the team in question did not use drugs; what had been mistakenly taken for a drug turned out to be nothing more than a spray to deter dryness of the mouth. Although no specific individual team members were mentioned the plaintiff contended that as a member of the team, and one who was rather well known, this claim reflected back upon him personally. The courts agreed with the plaintiff and he was awarded a sum of $75,000.[6]

Obviously, as a result of these legal actions, an individual who writes or makes quotable statements regarding athletes, coaches or officials should use extreme discretion in his selection of words. If one is not positive of the true facts then one might better hesitate before making a statement.

Injury to a Coach

Under present circumstances most coaching personnel have some type of accident insurance, provided either by themselves or by the school district. If a coach is injured in the carrying out of his duties he is usually covered by some type of insurance.

The normal reaction for a coach would be to avoid suing his employer, even if he could prove negligence. The natural tendency would be to avoid making it uncomfortable for his employer. In school districts that do carry liability insurance it would undoubtedly be perfectly legal for a coach to collect for an injury if there were negligence. In many situations, however, the coach might well be the individual responsible for a particular area where the injury occurred and he could certainly not sue for injuries which were the result of his own negligence.

There is a case on record in which a principal had as an indicated duty the responsibility for selecting a basketball team to represent his school. While performing this function as a coach, the principal was injured and collected damages.[7]

---

[6] *Fawcett Publications, Inc. vs. Morris,* 377 P. (2d) 42 (Oklahoma, 1962).
[7] *Milwaukee vs. Industrial Commission,* 160 Wisconsin 238.

In another similar case an assistant coach was struck by a wildly thrown ball during baseball practice and instituted legal action. The courts found that coaches as well as players assume a certain degree of risk in participating in such an activity and it was not a case of negligence.[8]

Hiring Sports Officials

The hiring of qualified sports officials is not only an ethical responsibility of the athletic director, but a legal responsibility as well. Although there seems to be no litigation involving the utilization of unqualified officials it would be very possible that this could be the basis for such an action.

The registration and certification of sports officials first took place in the Middle West in the 1920's. Since that time this practice has spread throughout the country and it is doubtful if there is any section remaining that does not utilize such a program. Officials' organizations have been formed in order to guarantee proficient and consistent performances by their members. In most instances these groups demand that a member work through various levels of certification and indicate by both written and practical testing programs they are capable of handling athletic contests. These groups have developed and have attempted to maintain high standards in order for an individual to be certified as a qualified official.

Certification does not necessarily guarantee outstanding officials, but the presence of an incompetent official under this program would be the exception rather than the rule. After having undergone training and testing there is no doubt the typical individual will become more proficient in his area of specialization. Once again the court can only judge legal actions by the rule rather than the exception.

---

[8] *McGee vs. Board of Education of New York City,* 16 App. Div. 2d 99 (New York, 1962).

A certified official must be considered as being much more capable than one who has not had such training. As a result, the use of a non-certified official could indicate to the court that his qualifications would be in question. Subjective judgment might indicate otherwise but the facts stand for themselves.

Assuming an athlete is injured in a contest in which there is an unqualified official, the plaintiff would immediately have a basis for a claim of negligence. Unqualified persons have been used in the past as officials in athletic contests and this would have provided fertile territory for legal action if a player were injured. In the past few years, however, there has been a definite decrease in this malpractice and one of the main reasons is probably due to the insistence of certified officials by state athletic associations.

Although varsity sports in almost instances are officiated by qualified persons, there are numerous instances where athletic activities below the varsity level are officiated by unqualified individuals. This is an area where the school district could well be leaving itself extremely vulnerable to legal action in the case of an injury. At the present time there is considerable variation of opinions on the advisability of junior high school athletics. With many such programs teetering close to elimination this is where some of the poorest officiating practices appear. Unqualified adults and sometimes even high school students are used as officials. With the situation as it exists, this is one area where qualified officials are a dire necessity.

Payment of Officials

In several cases already mentioned there have been variations in legal opinions regarding particular aspects which involve athletics. The payment of officials presents a similar variation in interpretations.

At the outset, the funds from which officials may receive

payment will depend upon the particular educational laws under which a school functions. In some states, as mentioned earlier, it is illegal to use public funds to finance any phase of the athletic program, which may include equipment, awards and officials. In this situation it would be necessary, therefore, to make payment to officials from the fund into which the gate receipts are deposited—the athletic association, athletic department, or whatever it may be called. On the other hand, in those states which do allow for payment of athletic program expenses from public money this expenditure will probably be legal. In some instances the school board is limited as to what it may expend for the athletic program. It may be allowed to purchase athletic equipment, but cannot purchase awards. It is also possible that public money cannot be spent for the payment of officials and that such expenses must therefore be taken from the gate receipts.

In New York it was not until a few years ago that the payment of officials was made a legal expenditure for a school board. In many situations it was found that in order to have a broad athletic program it was desirable to include activities which would supply no gate receipts due to their nature. In order to obtain competent officials for such activities it would have been necessary for other activities to provide financial support. If the income from the gate-receipt-producing activities was not sufficient to provide the necessary funds for officials in these other activities, the non-revenue-producing activities were either eliminated or had to get along with volunteer officials, who often proved to be very unsatisfactory. By making it legal for the board of education to make payment for such officials the breadth of the program did not have to be limited.

In this area of payments to officials there has been an inconsistency in interpretations and it would be wise for those responsible for making such payments to verify the legality of such a situation. This problem arises when an activity is postponed or interrupted by inclement weather or other unpredictable factors. This possibility predominates in certain activities such as baseball but could occur in almost any athletic contest. The officials may report for a contest, only to find that it has been postponed or cancelled for one reason or another. Or, on the other hand, the contest is interrupted by weather conditions which make it impossible to complete the regulation amount of time. Outdoor activities are most often considered as being prone to such situations but they can occur with indoor activities due to a number of factors.

When such an emergency does arise the officials' organizations usually have specific regulations to meet the unexpected. In some instances the officials receive half payment if they make the trip to the site of the contest, while in other cases they may receive full payment. This problem was presented in a recent athletic association meeting and a legal interpretation was requested. A representative of the State Education Department indicated it would be illegal to make any payment to officials, except for mileage expense, since an educational institution could not pay for a service which was not rendered. Thus the regulations of officials' organizations would appear to have been in direct opposition to that of the education department. This matter was brought before an athletic council, which represented the schools in one area of a state, and the chairman chose to verify the interpretation with the legal counsel of the state athletic association. According to the legal interpretation by the association's lawyer, the hiring of officials for an athletic contest is a contractual agreement, whether it be on a legal contract form or simply oral. Since the officials have fulfilled their obligation to the best of their ability and have no control over the weather or other factors, then the school, which had entered into this contract, is obligated to pay for such a service.

There are no litigations in this area and it would therefore be advisable for athletic coaching personnel to ascertain the specific regulations under which they are expected to function. If there is a variation in opinion, as there was here, it would be advisable to have the situation clarified before taking any positive action.

14

Future Trends

AS WAS MENTIONED AT THE START OF THIS BOOK, THE MATTER of statutes and legal interpretations is a constantly fluctuating situation. Circumstances will change as modern schools are constructed and these structures should be basically safe. Therefore the causes of many accidents can be directed at human error rather than inefficient and aged structures. It is common knowledge that attitudes change and court and jury judgments more and more reflect the opinion that the school district and its personnel are obligated to provide a safe atmosphere for the students. A situation which may have been considered as unpredictable in the past may no longer be held as such due to improved facilities and the emphasis upon inspection for safe conditions.

It is somewhat difficult to predict with any degree of certainty the exact legal changes which will take place within the next several years, but there have been several legal opinions which were indicative of the changing attitudes of judges and courts in legal actions. Some of these proved to be a complete reversal of former legal attitudes.

Removal of Immunity

It would appear as though the school districts throughout the nation will not retain their immunity from legal action for any length of time. In many states this concept of legal immunity was considered obsolete several years ago and was stricken from the statutes, or reversed by court judgment. Within the past few years there have been a number of states which have eliminated this tort immunity as a protection for schools. The original purpose of immunity was to protect the school districts from large financial losses, but the purchase of liability insurance has removed this danger to a large degree. In some states there is no limit to the amount of damages which can be claimed and it is necessary for the school districts to maintain high liability insurance coverage. In other instances the courts have indicated immunity should be removed to the extent of such liability coverage.

Illinois, Oregon, Wisconsin and Minnesota have only recently eliminated immunity from school districts. In some instances these states have used other court judgments as precedent-setting in nature and indicated their school districts should not be considered different from school districts in other states. Courts in Michigan and Pennsylvania have indicated they would definitely have abrogated immunity in certain litigations if it had not been for existing legislation. Many court opinions clearly indicate immunity should no longer apply and that such protection was obviously obsolete under present circumstances.

In some states the elimination of tort immunity will prove to be much more difficult as this protection is guaranteed under certain State Constitutions. In order for a change a Constitutional amendment, a much more complex procedure than the abrogation of a statute, would be necessary. Although many states do hold to immunity for school districts a number of such districts do purchase liability insurance. This would seem to indicate the officers of such school districts do feel immunity might possibly be removed and with such an eventuality they feel the district should be protected.

Increase in "Save Harmless" Protection

There are several reasons why there will be an increase in the number of states providing "save harmless" provisions for their teachers. Even though a school district may be immune this does not mean that an individual teacher is immune. As larger and larger claims are made teachers will become more concerned and those individuals involved in athletics will be a prime target for such litigations. In order to provide school personnel with a degree of security the school districts should feel obligated to protect such individuals from large financial losses.

With the tendency toward the elimination of immunity there may be an increase in the number of claims. If it can be proven a particular individual rather than the school district or its officers was responsible for the negligent situation those responsible for activities will become somewhat apprehensive. Once again the attitude should be that a teacher, whether he be a coach or some other person, must be protected if he is performing some activity which is within the scope of his responsibility.

In those states which do have "save harmless" provisions many have it on a permissive basis. Since the attitudes at the local level will vary considerably—some strongly in favor, while others just as strongly opposed—it would be advisable to have the "save harmless" provisions made mandatory so all teachers in a particular state would be provided with the same protection.

Increase in the Number of Litigations

There will probably be a tendency for the number of legal actions against the school districts or its employees to increase within the next several years. The present attitude would seem to be that students should attend school under extremely safe conditions. This appears to be somewhat of a change from the previous attitude whereby it was felt the youngster was fortunate in being able to attend school and if he was injured in some way it was not proper to sue an institution which was providing such an opportunity. With the educational systems now geared for attendance by all youngsters and mandated by law, in most cases, it should be the responsibility of the school to guarantee their pupils' safety. As was mentioned earlier, new school construction has eliminated many of the hazards that existed when there were obsolete buildings and facilities. Since safe planning has eliminated many of the preexisting hazards, then many of these dangerous situations are the result of individual negligence rather than poor environment.

It would seem the majority of the legal actions mentioned in this book took place in what might be considered larger school districts. There are basic reasons for such a situation. As the number of students served increases there will be an increase in the number of parents who consider an injury the basis for legal action. The number of individuals who would consider legal action against a school district after an injury is directly proportional to the number of students enrolled. Naturally this is also affected by the statutes of the state.

The tendency at the present time is to combine smaller school districts into larger units. Educationally it is felt that such action results in broader programs and more efficient utilization of teachers and facilities. This would have a dual relationship to the public attitude in litigations agaist the school district. As was just mentioned, an increase in enrollment in an educational institution will increase the number of people who would consider it proper to name the school district or an employee in a legal action. Another important aspect, all too often forgotten, is the personal relationship the public feels toward the school. In a small district there would be more rapport between the parents and the faculty, the administration and the school board. In case of an injury to a student the parents would be rather apprehensive in naming a member of the community in a legal action. It is doubtful if the members of a smaller community would look with approval upon such a suit, particularly if the individual involved had been accepted as a satisfactory employee of the school district. In the same vein, the school district is supported largely by local finances and any legal action would result in an increased expense for the district, which would influence the pocket book of every individual in the community. The impersonality of the larger school district has resulted in a reduction of this attitude and thus an increase in the number of legal actions.

Larger Financial Settlements

It would appear as though the general attitude toward the capabilities of children, both mental and physical, have changed. Previously a youngster was criticized for his folly when he was injured due to his own lack of foresight. It would seem at present, however, the courts feel the youngsters are extremely incapable of thinking or acting in a reasonable manner. Several of the court actions mentioned in this book would seem to bear this out.

In the legal action illustrated earlier, a youngster was told to remain inactive while the coach was out of the gymnasium caring for an injured student. In disobeying the coach's instructions the youngster was seriously injured and in the ensuing court case received a settlement of $1¼ million. Obviously the youngster chose to ignore the coach's orders but this had no bearing on the outcome of the case. Similarly, those court decisions which indicated it was improper for a youngster to perform a particular activity would seem to indicate a teacher or a coach must expect too much of his charges. Even though a coach may feel that a particular movement is well within the ability of the athlete the court decision may disagree with his opinion.

Large financial settlements are not unusual in legal actions involving youngsters. The present trend is toward greater sympathy for children and teenagers than would be exhibited in similar claims by adults. This is quite true in situations where the decision involves a judge, but is even more so when a jury becomes involved.

Increase in Slander and Libel Cases

Within the past few years there has been a tremendous increase in the number of slander and libel cases involving individuals concerned with athletics. This tendency may be due to the recognition by those involved in athletics that publications have no right to be as critical of their actions as they had been. It is not only the criticism of their actions but what might be inferred. In some instances their actions might have been open to public censure but some writers obviously made certain assumptions which were not true, or they may have reflected upon the character of the individual. In doing so they have left themselves wide open for slander charges.

There also seems to have been a relaxation on the censoring of articles by publishers. It would seem the more startling the article the more interested was the public. If such a publication could increase its circulation by a dramatic revelation in athletics then it might be willing to take a chance on libel or slander suits. If such a gamble has paid off for the publishers there might possibly be an increase in such articles, but conversely, if these litigations have proven to be financially damaging then there may be a revision of such a policy.

Results of the Trends

Assuming the aforementioned trends do develop, what will be the eventual outcomes? With the elimination of immunity, the increase in the number of cases and the increase in the financial settlements, coaches and other school personnel will become more and more cognizant of the causes and the results of litigations involving school districts. Professional publications and professional meetings are replete with discussions on the legal aspects of school functions. The colleges and universities are increasing the amount of information presented to their students in this area and new teachers are often more familiar with these situations than are some of those who have been in the field for some length of time. In addition to these sources of information the newspapers frequently carry stories on legal actions involving school districts and are particularly interested in presenting the facts on cases involving athletics since this area is of considerable interest to the general public.

Due to this increased emphasis and the previously mentioned trends, coaches are going to be more concerned with the elimination of hazards which might cause legal actions against them or the school district. As they attempt to eliminate negligence-producing situations, they will be moving in the direction of avoiding accidents. The fear of being involved in a litigation will lead to a safer atmosphere in athletic participation.

In conclusion, the following remarks of Attorney Harry N. Rosenfield, as he spoke to the National Conference on Accident Prevention in Physical Education, Athletics and Recreation in 1963, would seem appropriate:

The rule of governmental immunity for school accidents should be abolished. This is necessary not only in order to protect the innocent injured person, but also to encourage schools to avoid preventable accidents.

With these objectives in mind, and speaking only for myself, I propose to you and the schoolmen of America the following three-point program:

1. abolition of the doctrine of governmental immunity for school accidents, by legislation if necessary. School boards should be liable for their own negligence and for the negligence of their employees in the course of employment;

2. authorization of school boards to purchase all necessary and appropriate insurance to cover such liability; and

3. establishment or continuation of a first rate safety and accident prevention program in every school of this nation, in order to eliminate or substantially to curtail accidents and consequent problems of school liability.

In my judgment, such a program would not only do justice to all involved, but would also make schools safer throughout the United States.[1]

---

[1] Rosenfield, Harry N. *Legal Liability for School Accidents.* Remarks to the National Conference on Accident Prevention in Physical Education, Athletics and Recreation, Washington, D.C., Dec. 7, 1963.

List of Legal Actions

Chapter 1

Stone vs. Arizona State Highway Commission, 381 p. 2nd
107, (Arizona, 1963).

Molitor vs. Kaneland Community Unity District, 18, Illinois 2d 11, 163 N.E. 2d 89 to 96 (Illinois, 1959).

*Tesone vs. School District No. RE-2 in the County of
Boulder,* 384 P. (2d) 82 (Colorado, 1963).

Buck, et. al. vs. McLean, et. al., 115 So. (2d) 764 (Florida,
1959).

Richards vs. School District, 348, Michigan 490, 83 N.W.
643, (1957).

Chapter 2

Stone vs. Arizona State Highway Commission, 381 P. 2nd
107, (Arizona, 1963).

Molitor vs. Kaneland Community Unity District, 18, Illinois 2d 11, 163 N.E. 2d 89 to 96 (Illinois, 1959).

Chapter 3

*Garber vs. Central High School District, No. 1 of the Town
of Sharon,* 251 App. Div. 214, 295 N.Y.S. 850 (New
York, 1937).

Gardner vs. State of New York, 281 N.Y. 212.

Stanley Miller, et. al. vs. Board of Education of the Borough of Chatham, N.J. Sup. Ct. L. Div., No. L-7241
—63 (New Jersey, 1964).

Kidwell vs. School District No. 300, Whitman County, 335
P. (2d) 805 (Washington, 1959).

Fein vs. Board of Education of New York City, 111 N.E.
(2d) 742 (New York, 1953).

Domino vs. Mercurio, 234 N.Y.S. (2d) 1011 (New York,
1962).

Germond vs. Board of Education of New York City, 10
App. Div. 2d 139, 197 N.Y. Supp. 2d 548 (New York,
1960).

Underhill vs. Alameda Elementary School District, 133
Cal., App. 24 P (2d) (California, 1933).

Hale vs. Davies, 70 S.E. (2d) 923 (Georgia, 1952).

Sayers vs. Ranger, 83A. (2d) 775 (New Jersey, 1951).

Kaufman vs. City of New York, 214 N.Y.S. (2d) 767 (New
York, 1961).

Bellman vs. San Francisco High School, 11 California (2d)
576.

Gardner vs. State of New York 281 N.Y. 212.

Clark vs. Board of Education, 304 N.Y. 488, 109 N.E. 2d
73 (New York, 1952).

Charonnat vs. San Francisco Unified School District, 133
P. (2d) 643 (California, 1943).

Graff vs. N.Y.C. Board of Education, 283 N.Y. 24, 258 App.
Div. 813, 15 N.Y. Supp. (2d) 941 (1939).

Purkis vs. Walthamstown Borough Council, 151 Law
Times Reports 30.

Curicio vs. City of New York, 275 N.Y. 20, 9 N.E. (2d)
760 (1937).

Rodriques vs. San Jose Unified School District, 157 Cal.
App. 2d 842, 322 P. 2d 70 (California, 1958).

Bauer vs. Board of Education of the City of New York, 140
N.Y.S. (2d) 167 (New York, 1955).

Wright vs. San Bernardino High School District, 121 Cal.
App. Bd. 342, 263 P. 2d 25 (California, 1953).

Feuerstein vs. Board of Education, 202 N.Y. Supp. 2d 524
(1960), aff'd 13 App. Div. 2d 503, 214 N.Y. Supp. 2d
654 (1961).

Keesee vs. Board of Education of City of New York, 235
N.Y.S. (2d) 300 (New York, 1962).

Chapter 4

Bellman vs. San Francisco High School District.

Kerby vs. Elk Grove High School District, 36 P. (2nd) 431, (California, 1934).

Morris vs. Union High School District, 294 Pac. 998 (Washington, 1931).

Duda vs. Gaines, 79 A. (2d) 695 (New Jersey, 1951).

Guerri vs. Tyson, 24A (2d) 468 (Pennsylvania, 1942).

Pirkle vs. Oakdale Union School District, 253 P. (2d) 1 (California, 1953).

Sayers vs. Ranger, 83 A (2d) 775 (New Jersey, 1951).

Orgando vs. Carquinez Grammar School District, 24 Cal. App. (2d) 567, 75 P. (2d) 641 (1938).

Welch vs. Dunsmuir Joint Union High School District, 326, P. (2d) 633 (California, 1958).

Jarrett vs. Goodall, 168 S.E. 763 (West Virginia).

Chapter 5

Martini vs. School District of Olyphant.

Rapisardi vs. Board of Education of New York City, 272 N.Y.S. 360 (1934).

Bard vs. Board of Education of New York City, 140 N.Y. Supp. 2d 850 (New York, 1955).

In re. German Township School Directors, 46 D & C 562 (Pennsylvania, 1942).

McNair vs. District No. 1 of Cascade County et. al., 87 Montana 423, 288 p. 188 (1930).

Galloway vs. School District of Borough of Prospect Park, 331 Pa. 48, 200 A 99 (Pennsylvania, 1938).

Brine vs. City of Cambridge, 265 Massachusetts 452, 164 N.E. 2nd 619 (1929).

Bridge vs. Board of Education of City of Los Angeles 38 Pac. (2nd) 199 (California).

Mokovich vs. Independent School District, 177 Minnesota 466, 225 N.W. 292.

Katz vs. Board of Education of City of New York, 162 App. Div. 132.

Spencer vs. School District No. 1, Oregon, 254, Pac. 357.

Bradley vs. Board of Education of City of Oneonta, 276 NYS 622; 243 A.D. 651 (New York).

Kattershinsky vs. Board of Education of New York City, 212 N.Y.S. 424 (New York).

Bush vs. City of Norwalk, 122 Connecticut 426.

Kelly vs. New York City Board of Education, 191 App. Div. 251 (New York).

Freund vs. Oakland Board of Education, 82 P. (2d) 197, (California, 1938).

Donohue vs. Board of Education of Mt. Pleasant, N.Y., N.Y. Law Journal, Oct. 19, 1938, P. 1204.

Streickler vs. New York, 15 App. Div. 2d 927, 225 N.Y. Supp. 2d 602 (1962), rev'd 13 N.Y. 2d 716, 191 N.E. 2d 903 (1963).

Longo vs. New York City Board of Education, 225, N.Y., 719.

Chapter 6

Adonnino vs. Village of Mt. Morris, 12 N.Y.S. (2nd) 658.

Barnecut vs. Seattle School District No. 1, 389 P. 2d 904.

Weldy vs. Oakland High School District of Alameda County, 65 P. (2d) 851 (California, 1937).

Brown vs. City of Oakland, 124 P. (2d) 369 (California, 1942).

Watson vs. School District, 324 Mich. 1, 36 N.W. 2d 195 (1949).

Ingerson vs. Shattucks School, Minnesota, 239 N.W. 667 (1931).

Thompson vs. Board of Education, City of Millville, 79 A. (2d) 100 (New Jersey, 1951).

Reed vs. Rhead County, 225 S.W. (2nd) 49 (Tennessee, 1949).

Sawaya vs. Tucson High School District No. 1, 281 P. (2d) 105 (Arizona, 1955).

Kellam vs. School Board of City of Norfolk, 202 Va. 252, 117 S.E. 2d 96 (1960).

Larsen vs. Independent School District of Kane, 223 Iowa, 691.

Richards vs. School District of Birmingham, 348 Mich. 490, 83 N.W. 2d 643.

George vs. University of Minnesota Athletic Association, 107 Minn. 424.

Scott vs. University of Michigan Athletic Association, 152 Michigan 664; 116 N.W. 624.

Juntilla vs. Everett School District No. 24, Washington; 35 Pac. (2nd) 78.

Chapter 7

Schmidt vs. Blair, 203 Iowa 1016, 213 N.W. 593 (1927).

Bear vs. Board of Education of No. Summit School District, et. al., 81 Utah 51, 16 P. 2d 900 (1932).

Parr vs. Board of County Commissioners, 207 Md. 91, 113 A. 2d 397 (Maryland, 1955).

Phillips vs. Hardgrove, 161 Washington 121 (296). 559 (1931).

Davidson vs. Hoarne, 71 S.E. (2d) 464 (Georgia, 1952).

Van Cleave vs. Illini Coach Co., N.E. (2d) 398 (Illinois, 1951).

People vs. Casey, 33 N.Y.S. (2d) 1, 263 App. Div. 342 (1942).

Beardsell vs. Tilton School, 200 A 783, (New Hampshire, 1938).

Roberts vs. Baker, 192 S.E. 104 (Georgia, 1938).

Lewis vs. Halbert, 67 S.W. (2d) 430 (Texas, 1933).

Harrison vs. McVeight, 5 S.E. (2d) 76 (Georgia, 1939).

Wynn vs. Gaudy, 197 S.E. 527 (Virginia, 1938).

Hibbs vs. Independent School District of Green Mountain, 218 Iowa 841, 251, N.W. 606 (1933).

Betts vs. Jones et. al., 166 S.E. 589 (No. Carolina).

Roberts vs. Baker, 57 Ga. 733, 196 S.E. 104 (1938).

Krasner vs. Harper, 90 Ga. App. 128, 82 S.E. 2d 267 (1954).

Gorton vs. Doty, 57 Idaho, 792, 69 P. 2d 136 (1937).

Truitt vs. Gaines, 318 F. (2d) 461 (Delaware, 1963).

Kitzel vs. Athkenson, 245 P. (2d) 170 (Kansas, 1952).

Fessenden vs. Smith, 124 N.W. (2d) 554 (Iowa, 1964).

Chapter 8

Livingston vs. New Mexico College of A & M Arts, 328 P (2d) 79 (New Mexico, 1958).

Supler vs. School District of North Franklin Township, 182 A (2d) 535 (Pennsylvania, 1962).

Board of Education of the County of Raleigh vs. Commercial Casualty Insurance Co., 116 W.Va. 503, 182 S.E. 87 (1935).

Vendrell vs. School District No. 26 Malheur County, 360 P. (2d) 282 (Oregon, 1961).

Thomas vs. Broadlands Community Consolidated School District, 348 Illinois App. 567, 109 N.E. 2d 636 (1952).

Chapter 9

Kinzer vs. Torns, 129 Iowa 441, 105 N.W. 686, 3 L.R.A. 496.

O'Rourke vs. Walker, 102 Conn. 130, 128 Atl. 25, 41 A.L.R.

Dresser vs. District Board.

Baker vs. Stevenson, 189 N.E. (2d) 181 (Ohio, 1962).

Starkey vs. Board of Education of Davis County School District, 381 P. (2d) 718 (Utah, 1963).

Chapter 10

LeValley vs. Stanford, 272 App. Div. 183, 70 N.Y.S. 2d 460 (1947).

Reynolds vs. State, 207 Misc. 693, 141 N.Y. Supp. 2d 615 (New York, 1955).

Brooks vs. Board of Education of City of New York, 205 N.Y.S. (2d) 777 (New York, 1960).

Vendrell vs. School District No. 26C Malheuser County, 376 P 2d 406 (Oregon, 1962).

Chapter 11

Morrison vs. Roberts, 183 Okl. 359, 82 Pac. 2d 1023 (Oklahoma, 1938).

Chapter 12

Sult vs. Gilbert, 3 Southern 2d 729 (Florida, 1941).

University Interscholastic League vs. Midwestern University, 250 Southwestern 587, (Texas, 1953).

State of North Dakota vs. North Central Association of Colleges and Secondary Schools, CCA 7, 99 Fec. 2nd, 697, (North Dakota, 1938).

Morrison vs. Roberts, 183 Okl. 359, 82 Pac. 1023 (Oklahoma, 1938).

Miller vs. Waldorf, Court of Appeals, Third Appellate Judicial District of Ohio, Hancock County, June 19, 1952.

West Virginia Secondary School Activities Commission vs. Wagner, 102 S.E., 2nd 901 (West Virginia, 1958).

Chapter 13

Southwestern Broadcasting Company vs. Oil Center Broadcasting Company, 210 S.W. 2nd (Texas, 1947).

Colorado High School Activities Association vs. Uncompangre Broadcasting Co., 134 Colorado 131, 300 P. 2d 698 (1956).

McGrath vs. Burkhard (California, 1955).

Pease vs. Millcreek Township School District, 195 A (2nd) 104 (Pennsylvania, 1963).

Fawcett Publications, Inc. vs. Morris, 377 P. (2d) 42 (Oklahoma, 1962).

Milwaukee vs. Industrial Commission, 160 Wisconsin 238.

McGee vs. Board of Education of New York City, 16 App. Div. 2d 99 (New York, 1962).

Bibliography

Books

AMERICAN ASSOCIATION OF HEALTH, PHYSICAL EDUCATION AND RECREATION. *Coaches Handbook*. Washington: National Education Association, 1960.

BILIK, STEPHEN E. *The Trainers Bible*. New York: T. J. Reed Co., 1946.

FORSYTHE, CHARLES. *Administration of High School Athletics*. Englewood Cliffs, N.J.: Prentice-Hall, Inc., 1959.

FORSYTHE, CHARLES. *The Athletic Director's Handbook*. Englewood Cliffs, N.J.: Prentice-Hall, Inc., 1956.

GALLAGHER, E. C. and PEERY, REX. *Wrestling* (rev. ed.). New York: A. S. Barnes Co., 1950.

GAUERKE, W. E. *Legal and Ethical Responsibilities of School Personnel*. Englewood Cliffs, N.J.: Prentice-Hall, Inc., 1959.

GRIEVE, ANDREW. *Directing High School Athletics*. Englewood Cliffs, N.J.: Prentice-Hall, Inc., 1963.

HAGENY, WILLIAM J. *Handbook of New York State Education Law*. Albany: New York State School Boards Association, Inc., 1964.

HAMILTON, ROBERT and MORT, PAUL. *The Law and Public Education*. Brooklyn: Foundation Press, 1959.

KENNEY, J. B. *A Practical Law Guide for New York Teachers*. Suffern, N.Y.: J. B. Kenney, 1952.

LEIBEE, HOWARD. *Liability for Accidents in Physical Education, Athletics and Recreation*. Ann Arbor, Michigan: Ann Arbor Publishers, 1952.

LEIBEE, HOWARD. *Tort Liability for Injuries to Pupils*. Ann Arbor, Michigan: Campus Publishers, 1965.

171

LLOYD, G. C., DEAVER, F. R. and EASTWOOD, W. B. *Safety In Athletics.* Philadelphia: W. B. Saunders, 1939.

McCANN, L. E. and LARSON, E. L. *School District Liability for Damage Suits.* Tucson, Arizona: Bureau of School Services, College of Education, The University of Arizona, 1963.

National Federation of State High School Athletic Associations Handbook. Chicago: National Federation of High School Athletic Associations, 1964–65.

NATIONAL EDUCATION ASSOCIATION. *The Physical Education Instructor and Safety.* High School Series. Bulletin No. 2. Washington: N.E.A. Research Division, 1948.

NATIONAL EDUCATION ASSOCIATION. *The Pupil's Day in Court: Review of 1963.* Washington: N.E.A. Research Division, March, 1964.

NATIONAL EDUCATION ASSOCIATION. *The Teacher's Day in Court: Review of 1963.* Washington: N.E.A. Research Division, March, 1964.

NATIONAL EDUCATION ASSOCIATION. *Who is Liable for Pupil Injuries?* Washington: N.E.A. Research Division, 1963.

NOLTE, M. C. and LINN, J. P. *School Law for Teachers.* Danville, Illinois: Interstate Printers and Publishers, 1963.

PUNKE, HAROLD. *The Law and Liability in Pupil Transportation.* Chicago: University of Chicago Press, 1943.

REMMLEIN, MADALINE. *School Law.* Danville, Illinois: Interstate Printers and Publishers, 1962.

ROSENFIELD, HARRY N. *Liability for School Accidents.* New York: Harper and Bros., 1940.

Magazine Articles

BLYTH, C. S. and LOVINGOOD, B. W. "Harmful Effects of Crash Dieting." *The Athletic Journal,* (May, 1963), p. 30.

DOSCHER, NATHAN and WALKE, NELSON. "The Status of Liability for School Physical Education Accidents and

Its Relationship to the Health Program" *A.A.H.P.E.R. Research Quarterly*, Volume 23, No. 3 (October, 1952). p. 280.

DOYLE, KENNETH. "Why Sports' Seasons?" *The New York State Journal of Health, Physical Education and Recreation*, Volume 15, No. 2 (Winter, 1962–63), P. 30. (from speech to National Federation Meeting, July, 1962).

GILES, JOHN. "Liability of Coaches and Athletic Instructors." *The Athletic Journal*, Volume XLII, Number 6 (February, 1962), p. 18.

GOLD, S. Y. and GOLD, G. F. "First Aid and Legal Liability." *The Journal of Health, Physical Education and Recreation*, Volume 34, No. 1 (January, 1963), p. 42.

JORDAN, WILLIAM. "Liability and School Athletics." *The Athletic Journal*, (September, 1964), p. 76.

MURPHY, ROBERT J. "Witholding Participants from Sports and Return to Competition." *The Wisconsin Medical Journal*, Vol. 61 (Sept., 1962), p. 417. (from a speech to the State Medical Society, Milwaukee, May 9, 1962).

"New Law Section." *Journal of New York State School Boards Association*, Volume 24, No. 2 (June, 1960), p. 18.

RASCH, P. J. and KROLL, W. "Safe Wrestling" *The Journal of Health, Physical Education and Recreation*, Vol. 36, No. 3 (March, 1965), p. 32.

RUSSELL, JAMES. "Medical Aspects of Sports." *The New York State Journal of Health, Physical Education and Recreation*, Vol. 15, No. 3 (Spring, 1963), p. 40. (from a speech to National Federation Meeting, July, 1962).

"School Laws and Teacher Negligence." *N.E.A. Research Bulleting*, Volume 40, No. 3 (October, 1962), p. 75.

"Scoreboard." *Sports Illustrated*, Volume 23, No. 2 (July, 12, 1965), p. 11.

SHROYER, GEORGE F. "Coaches Legal Liability for Athletic Injuries." *The Athletic Journal*, Volume 34, No. 4 (December, 1964), p. 18.

ZIMMERMAN, L. L. "Coaches Are Liable." *The Texas Coach,* (April, 1959), p. 10.

Newsletter

"Some Legal Aspects of Athletics." *Physical Education Newsletter,* Croft Educational Services, New London, Connecticut, Letter 5, Vol. 6 (Oct. 27, 1961).

"Political Football." *Physical Education Newsletter,* Croft Educational Services, New London, Connecticut, Letter 10, Vol. 6 (January 27, 1962).

"Accidents in Physical Education: How to Avoid Them— Their Effect on the Physical Education Teacher and the Curriculum." *Physical Education Newsletter.* Croft Educational Services, New London, Connecticut, Letter 15, Vol. 7 (March 27, 1963).

Pamphlets

BRIND, CHARLES. *Negligence.* Law Pamphlet No. 10, Law Division, New York State Education Department, Albany, N.Y.

First Aid Care of School Emergencies. The University of the State of New York, the State Education Department, Bureau of Health Services, Albany, N.Y., 1962.

Professional Papers

BRICKER, JOHN W. *Interpretations of State Law on Interscholastic Athletics.* Opinion #635. Attorney General of the State of Ohio, April 18, 1933.

LEIBEE, HOWARD C. *Legal Bases of Liability for Athletic Trainers.* The University of Michigan.

MURPHY, ROBERT J. and ASHE, WILLIAM F. *Sports and Climatic Conditions.* Ohio State University.

PATE, ROBERT. *Legal Liability for Athletic Injuries.* Director of H.P.E.R., Lockport, New York.

Remarks

Attorney General's Opinions, Wisconsin Interscholastic Athletic Association, 1949.

JEHU, JOHN P. *Report of the Statewide Conference For School District Directors of Health, Physical Education and Recreation.* Albany, N.Y., Nov. 15, 1962.

JOHNSON, HOWARD. *Digest of Court Cases Involving State High School Associations.* National Federation Meeting, Santa Barbara, California, 1958.

ROSENFIELD, HARRY N. *Legal Liability for School Accidents.* National Conference on Accident Prevention in Physical Education, Athletics and Recreation. Washington, D.C., Dec. 7, 1963.

Miscellaneous

Mutual Legal Aid Pact, Set II. National Federation of High School Athletic Associations, Chicago, Illinois.

Index

Accident insurance, 115–116; New York State Education Law, 116; premium payment, 115; required coverage, 116

Act of God, 21

Adhesive strapping (*see* Taping)

Alabama, 28; State Board of Adjustments, 28; statutes, 28

Alaska, 28; statutes, 28

Allergy, 74

All star games, 138

American Association of Health, Physical Education and Recreation, 58, 78, 115

American Medical Association, 76

Appeals to higher courts, 17

Areas, 50–53

Arizona, 24; abolishment of immunity, 24; liability insurance, 28; statutes, 28

Arkansas, 28; statutes, 28

Ashe, Dr. William, 76

Assigned duties, 53–55

Assumption of risk, 21, 45–46

Athletic awards, 128–131; legality of purchase, 128; limitations, 129; New York State Education Law, 128

Athletic budget, 84

Athletic contests: admission to, 98; ejection of spectators, 98

Athletic equipment manufacturers, 80

Athletic trainer: legal aspects, 79; legal liability, 79; legality of hiring, 78–79; physiotherapist, 79; role of, 78–79; treatment, 79

Attractive nuisance, 21, 91

Avoidance of accidents, 161

Balance beam, 89

Baseball: backstop, 93; bat, 94

Basketball, 25; overlapping courts, 52

Bleachers, 97–98; collapse, 97; construction, 97

Blyth, C. S., 76

Bonded common carriers, 102

Boxing, 124

177

Brain injuries, 64
Broadcasting athletic contests, 144–145

California, 29; liability insurance, 29; "safe place" statute, 29; statutes, 29
Camps, football, 49
Causative factor, 22, 46
Civil action, 22
Coercion, 65
Colorado, 29; immunity, 25; liability insurance, 29; State Education Association, 29; statutes, 29
Colorado High School Activities Association, 145
Common law, 22
Community team, 93
Comparative negligence, 22
Conditioning, 49–50
Connecticut, 29; liability insurance, 29; "save harmless" legislation, 29; statutes, 29
Constitution: Federal, 25; state, 25
Contact sports, 64
Contests: illegal number, 54; number, 54
Contributory negligence, 22
Courts, 87
Court judgement, 22, 24, 25
Court records, 17
Crash dieting, 77
Criminal action, 22

Definition of terms, 21–23
Dehydration, 77
Delaware, 29; liability insurance, 29; State Education Association, 29; statutes, 29
Diagnosis, 72

Diving, 48
Doctors, availability, 69
Drugs, 148–149
Drury, Robert, 47

Eligibility regulations, 117–122; local regulations, 117–118; married students, 121; state athletic associations, 133
Equal competition, 123–127; individual, 123; team, 125–127
Equipment, 80–87; baseball base, 82; baseball bat, 82; finance, 84–87; freshman teams, 80; head gear, 81; illegal use, 83; junior high teams, 80; junior varsity, 80; mouthpiece, 81–82
Equipment purchase, 82–84; bids, 83; collusion, 83; Massachusetts, 85–86; Montana, 85; Ohio, 86–87; Pennsylvania, 85

Facilities, 87–91; defective floor, 88; playground, 91; unsupervised, 91
Fellowship of Christian Athletes, 131
Fencing, protective, 95
Fields, 87
Financial responsibility, 74–75
Financial settlements, 159–160; attitude of courts, 159; increase, 161
First aid, 65–69; definition, 66; ethical procedures, 68; legal requirements, 68; movement of injured, 68
Florida, 29–30; Attorney General, 29–30; immunity, 25; liability insurance, 30; statutes, 29; Supreme Court, 138

Florida High School Athletic Association, 138
Football, 126
Foresight, 22, 42–45; in transportation, 102–103
Future trends, 155–162

Gallagher, E. C., 53
Georgia, 30; statutes, 30
Governmental function, 22, 88
Gymnasiums, 87
Gymnastics, 48

Hamilton, Robert, 85, 98, 101
Handball, 52–53
Hawaii, 30; liability insurance, 30; statutes, 30; Tort Liability Act, 30
Hazards, knowledge of, 87–88
Headstand, 48
Heat exhaustion, 49

Idaho, 30; liability insurance, 30; State Education Association, 30; statutes, 30
Illinois, 30–31; immunity, abolishment of, 24, 30; liability insurance, 31; State Constitution, 30–31; statutes, 30
Immunity, 17, 22, 111; changing attitude, 26; elimination, 16, 27, 155–156, 157, 161, 162
Indiana, 31; liability insurance, 31; statutes, 31
Individual judgement, 15
Inherent dangers, 43
Injunction, 22
Injuries: internal, 67; to coach, 149–150
In loco parentis, 22
Insurance, 111–116; malpractice, 74; transportation, 103

Insurance, accident, 75, 115–116 (*see also* Accident insurance) ; non-insurable, 62
Insurance, liability, 111–115, 156; illegal expenditure, 111, 113; individual coverage, 38, 115; legality, 38; mandated legislation, 111–112; permissive legislation, 112; purchase of, 162; spectators, 114; transportation, 112, 114
Interpretations, variations, 16
Iowa, 31; liability insurance, 31; State Education Department, 31; statutes, 31; Supreme Court, 101

Jehu, John F., 41, 42, 117
Junior high athletics, 48

Kansas, 31; liability insurance, 31; statutes, 31
Kentucky, 31; liability insurance, 31; statutes, 31
Kidney dysfunction, 77
Kroll, Walter, 78

Legal causation, 46
Legal changes, 155
Legal liability: attitude toward, 16; doctors, 72–74
Legal precedents, 14, 15, 17
Legal terms, 21–23 (*see also* Definition of terms)
Leibee, Howard, 27, 115
Liability, 22; avoidance of, 58–59
Libel, 147–149; increase in cases, 160
Litigation, 22; increase, 157–159, 161; size of schools, 158; small school district, 158
Locker rooms, 87, 90; supervision, 90

Lockers, 90

Louisiana, 31; liability insurance, 31; statutes, 31

Lovingood, R. W., 76

Maine, 31–32; liability insurance, 32; statutes, 31

Malfeasance, 22

Mandatory legislation, 23

Maryland, 32; State Education Association, 32; statutes, 32

Massachusetts, 32; liability insurance, 32; liability insurance for transportation, 32; "save harmless" legislation, 32; statutes, 32

Mats, 89

Medical aspects, 60–79

Medical assistance, 69–70

Michigan, 32; immunity, 25, 32; State Education Association, 32; statutes, 32; Supreme Court, 32

Midwestern University, 138

Minnesota, 32–33; immunity, removal of, 32–33; liability insurance, 33; "save harmless" legislation, 33; State Education Association, 33; statutes, 32; Supreme Court, 32

Miscellaneous legal problems, 144–154

Misfeasance, 23

Mississippi, 33; liability insurance, 33; States Claim Commission, 33; statutes, 33; transportation injuries, 33

Missouri, 33; statutes, 33

Montana, 33; liability insurance, 33; State Education Association, 33; statutes, 33

Mort, Paul, 85, 98, 101

Murphy, Dr. Robert, 76

Mutual Legal Aid Pact, 134–135

National Federation of Public High School Athletic Associations, 64, 72, 76, 134; athletic accident insurance, 115–116; origin, 134

National Federation of Public High School Athletic Associations Handbook, 115–116, 134

Nebraska, 33; liability insurance, 33; statutes, 33

Negligence, 23

New England Journal of Medicine, 76

New Hampshire, 34; liability insurance, 34; statutes, 34

New Jersey, 34; legal action, negligence, 43; liability insurance, 34; "save harmless" legislation, 34; statutes, 34

New Mexico, 34; liability insurance, 34; State Education Association, 34; statutes, 34

New York, 34; broadcasting games, 145; Education Law, 99, 146; liability insurance, 34; payment of officials, 152; "save harmless" legislation, 25, 34; State Constitution, 145; statutes, 34

New York State Department of Education, 65–66, 142; Board of Regents, 143; Bureau of Finance and Control, 84

New York State High School Athletic Protection Plan, 62

New York State Public High School Athletic Association, 142

Nevada, 33–34; athletic accident insurance, 34; liability insurance, 33–34; statutes, 33

Non-contact sports, 64

Non-feasance, 23

North Carolina, 34; liability insurance, 34; statutes, 34

North Dakota, 34–35; liability insurance, 34–35; statutes, 34

Ohio, 35; Attorney General, 137; liability insurance, 35; statutes, 35

Ohio High School Athletic Association, 137

Oklahoma, 35; liability insurance for transportation, 35; statutes, 35

Oklahoma High School Athletic Association, 140; award limitations, 130

Opinions of others, 57–58

Oregon, 35; liability insurance, 35; proprietary functions, 35; "save harmless" legislation, 35; State Education Association, 35; statutes, 35

Pancreatitis, acute, 77

Parental approval, 56

Parking lot, 95

Participants, number of, 50–53

Peery, Rex, 53

Pennsylvania, 35; liability insurance, 35; statutes, 35

Permissive legislation, 23

Physical defects, not reported, 60

Physical Education Newsletter, 66

Physical examinations, 60–64; athletic insurance, 62; cardiovascular disease, 64; completeness, 61–62; dislocating knee joint, 62; disqualifying conditions, 63; headaches, 64; head injury, 64; heart, 62; heart disease, 62; hernia, 62; mandate, 61; maturity, 64; nervous system, disease of, 64; non-insurable, 63; one eye, 62; orthopedic conditions, 64; paired organs, absence of, 64; paired organs, severe disease, 64; personal physician, 61; school physician, 61; unrevealed defects, 63; urinalysis, 62; vision, 62

Physiotherapy, 73

Practice sessions, 49; experimental program, 54; illegal, 49, 50, 54, 55

Precedents, 17, 23

Proprietary function, 23, 95–96; leasing of facilities, 96

Professional opinions, 47, 53

Public domain, 144

Public funds for athletic transportation, 101–102; Iowa, 101; Minnesota, 102; South Dakota, 102; Utah, 101

Public function, 22, 95–96 (*see also* Governmental function); charging admission, 95–96

Radiator, in gymnasium, 89

Rasch, Philip, 78

Ray, Kenneth, 47

Reinjury, 65

Release from doctor, 65

Respondea superior, 23

Responsibility, assumption of, 16

Rhode Island, 35; Attorney General, 35; statutes, 35

Rights of minors, 56

Roll, dive, 47

Rowdyism, 94

Rules, modification of, 49

Russell, Dr. James, 63, 72

"Safe place" legislation, 23

"Save harmless" legislation, 17, 23, 25, 38, 157; enactment of, 38; mandatory, 157; not applicable, 49–50; permissive, 38, 157

School bus drivers, 104; hiring, 106–107

School construction, 158

School nurse, at contests, 69

Scope of responsibility, 23, 27

Screening, protective, 93–94 (see also Fencing)

Scrimmages: inter-school, 50; practice, 54;

Shower facilities, 90

Skill, degree of, 47

Slander, 147–149; increase in cases, 160; publications, 148

Soccer, 125; line, 57; skills, 57–58

Somersault, 48

South Carolina, 35–36; liability insurance, transportation, 36; statutes, 35

South Dakota, 36; liability insurance, 36; "save harmless" legislation, 36; State Education Association, 36; statutes, 36

Spectators: assumption of risk, 93; injuries, 92–99

Sports officials: certified, 150–151; contractual agreement, 153; hiring, 150–151; interrupted contests, 153; junior high athletics, 151; legality of payment, 152; non-certified, 151; payment, 151–154; postponed games, 152–153; unqualified, 150

Springboard, 89–90

Standard procedures, 57

Stands, 97–98 (see also Bleachers)

State Athletic Associations, 13, 27, 54; award regulations, 130; control of high school athletics, 132; imposing fines, 136; legal actions, 137–143; legal aspects, 132–143; origin, 133; right to impose penalties, 135–136; State Education Department affiliated, 132; suspension from, 137; university directed, 132–133; voluntary membership, 132

State Education Departments, 27; liability insurance, 115; liability protection, 38

State Legal Divisions, 27

State syllabus, 57

Statutes, 23, 24, 25; changes, 16; existing, 17; standardization, 26; states, 26

Student, as supervisor, 42

Student teacher, 41–42; as coach, 42; as supervisor, 41–42; status, 41–42

Supervision, 39; bowling club, 147; competence, 40; extra-curricular activities, 146; football, 50–51; janitor, 40; numerical ratio, 51–52; playground, 51; qualifications, 39–42; swimming pool, 51

Syllabus, 57

Taping, 71; as treatment, 71–72; injury prevention, 71

Teacher, supervision assignments, 146–147

Teaching certificate, loss of, 50

Teams: freshman, 48; junior varsity, 48

Tennessee, 36; liability insurance, transportation, 36; statutes, 36

Tetanus, 73

Texas, 36; liability insurance, 36; State Education Association, 36; statutes, 36

Texas Interscholastic League, award limitations, 131

Tort, 23

Training, 49–50

Trampoline, 57

Transportation, 100–110; accidents, 100; governmental function, 106; "guest statute," 108–109, 110; imprudent speed, 105; negligence, 103–107; overloaded vehicles, 104; privately owned vehicles, 108–109; school owned vehicles, 103, 107; spectators, 104; team members, 104–105; violation of existing statutes, 104

Treatment, 72; head injuries, 73; heat lamps, 70; illegal, 70–72; internal medication, 70; termination of, 73; whirlpool, 70; written consent, 74

Trends, results of, 161–162

Unavoidable accident, 23

University Interscholastic League, 138, 139

University of Michigan Athletic Association, 97–98

University of Minnesota Athletic Association, 97

Unslaked lime, 88

Utah, 36; liability insurance, 36; State Education Association, 36; statutes, 36; Supreme Court, 101

Vermont, 36; liability insurance, 36; liability insurance for transportation, 36; State Education Association, 36; statutes, 36

Virginia, 36; liability insurance, 36; State Education Association, 36; statutes, 36

Voluntary participation, 45

Waiver forms, 56

Warning of dangers, 46

Washington, 37; liability insurance, 37; statutes, 37

Weight control, 75–78

West Virginia, 37; governmental function, 37; liability insurance, 37; State Education Association, 37; State Constitution, 37; statutes, 37

Wichita Falls School District, 138

Wisconsin, 37; athletic awards, 129–130; Attorney General, 118–120, 129, 135; immunity, abolishment of, 37; liability insurance, 37; liability insurance for transportation, 37; "safe place" statute, 37; statutes, 37

Wisconsin Interscholastic Athletic Association, 118

Witnesses, expert, 57

Wrestling, 53, 75–76, 123–124, 125; super-heavyweight class, 124; unlimited class, 124; weight classification, 123

Wyoming, 37; liability insurance, 37; liability insurance for transportation, 37; "save harmless" legislation, 37; statutes, 37

X ray, 73